P9-DTA-156

"Simply superb. A genuine model of Christian devotional writing—warm, enriching, and exciting application drawn from insightful expository and theological reflection on the biblical text. Each of these brief chapters is an absolute delight to read. This is joyful Christmastime reading for Christians of every age and experience. Very highly recommended."

FRED ZASPEL, Executive Editor, Books At a Glance; Adjunct Professor of Theology, The Southern Baptist Theological Seminary

"In this delightful book, Christopher Ash takes us slowly but surely through the real story of Christmas from Luke's Gospel, reflecting with insight and warmth on its deepest meaning and enabling us to both sing and pray with greater understanding and joy. A beautiful way to prepare our hearts for Christmas."

LEE GATISS, Director, Church Society

"Christopher Ash shows us the refreshing, startling realities that lie behind our Christmas festivities. Whether you're familiar with the story of the birth of Jesus or yet to be convinced it has any real relevance to life today, this will make you sit up, think again, and give thanks for these events that happened so long ago. I'm going to enjoy using it."

SAM ALLBERRY, Author, *Why Bother With Church?* and *Is God Anti-Gay?*

"Christopher Ash is a proven scholar with pastoral sensibilities. His Advent meditations will give substance to the season for you and your kin. As the world turns its attention to Christmas, even as much as it tries to cover it over with Santa and sentimentalities, it unavoidably invites Christ's people to commend him. Let's not blush and utter a few holiday trivialities. Let's give details and contours. Let's provide reasons for Christmas—which begins with feeding our own souls on the substance of the season. Open to these 24 meditations each day in December and let the fresh air of Christmas sanity return to your soul."

DAVID MATHIS, Executive Editor, desiringGod.org; Pastor, Cities Church, Minneapolis / St. Paul, Minnesota; Author, *Habits of Grace: Enjoying Jesus Through the Spiritual Disciplines*

"Christopher Ash has put together a wonderful resource for Advent. Engaging explorations of Luke's account of the birth of Jesus, a prayer to pray, a hymn to sing (if you dare) and room to record your own observations. We tried them around the dinner table and they worked. Recommended."

MARK THOMPSON, Principal, Moore College

"These devotionals are digestible: they will go down easily in the busy days of Advent. They are profound: they will go down deep. Most wonderfully, they are word-filled: they will feed us with the truth and beauty of the Scriptures, and of the Savior whose advent we celebrate."

KATHLEEN NIELSON, Author; Speaker

"A gem of a book: faithful to the text, sensitively applied, imaginatively illustrated, full of grace and wisdom, rich and deep in theology, and, most importantly, spiritually refreshing—it caused me to worship in my heart as I read."

JOHN SAMUEL, Senior Minister, Duke Street Church, Richmond, UK

"Christopher Ash has a gift from God of showing you clearly what is in Scripture which we so easily miss. It is no little thing to take familiar passages and handle them freshly, giving new insights into the wonder of who Jesus is. *Repeat the Sounding Joy* is full of warm, heart-searching application, terrific hymns and wonderful prayers."

PAUL LEVY, Minister, International Presbyterian Church Ealing, UK

"I can think of no better way to approach the Christmas season than reading the richly biblical and thoughtfully pastoral meditations in Christopher Ash's latest book. Ash always writes with an insightful sensitivity to the joys and sorrows, the hopes and fears of Christians, and these twenty-four meditations on the opening chapters of Luke's Gospel are no exception. The meditations unfold both the wonder and the challenge of the incarnation. Reading these brief chapters will inform and inspire. I have resolved to buy copies for my children and their families."

IAN HAMILTON, Trustee, Banner of Truth

REPEAT THE

SOUNDING JOY

thegoodbook
COMPANY

Repeat the Sounding Joy
© Christopher Ash 2019. Reprinted 2020, 2021.

Published by:
The Good Book Company

thegoodbook.com | thegoodbook.co.uk
thegoodbook.com.au | thegoodbook.co.nz | thegoodbook.co.in

Unless indicated, all Scripture references are taken from the Holy Bible, New International Version. Copyright © 2011 Biblica, Inc.TM Used by permission.

All rights reserved. Except as may be permitted by the Copyright Act, no part of this publication may be reproduced in any form or by any means without prior permission from the publisher.

Christopher Ash has asserted his right under the Copyright, Designs and Patents Act 1988 to be identified as author of this work.

ISBN: 9781784983789 | Printed in India

Design by André Parker

CONTENTS

INTRODUCTION

A dvent is a waiting game.

From here on in, most of us have got our minds set on Christmas. The children are waiting with great anticipation—come December 1st they will be peeling back the doors on their Advent calendars as they count down to the big day. The adults are waiting too as they get ready for the great celebrations—storing up food, buying presents, sending cards, planning get-togethers. Some of us love it; others find it a stress—but we can't avoid it. It's all about Christmas.

This book is written to help you set your mind on Christmas—not the day to come in two or three weeks but that glorious night in Bethlehem two thousand years ago. I want you to come with me through the opening two chapters of Luke's Gospel, in which Luke most vibrantly and wonderfully tells us of the birth of the Lord Jesus Christ. Each day we will focus on one thought from Luke's account; we will pause and meditate on that one thought. My hope is that you will arrive at the 25th of December with a heart that is thrilled by and thankful for the gift of the Lord Jesus.

So in the coming weeks we will be thinking about Christmas; but we are not waiting for Christmas. Instead, our meditations on Christmas will shape us to wait well for something even better.

Advent is a double-edged season. We think of it as the run-up to Christmas, but when the Christian church speaks of Advent, we mean something much grittier and more substantial. The word "advent" comes from the Latin word for "coming". And the New Testament speaks of Jesus coming into the world at two separate times. First—as will be the focus of our meditation in this devotional—his coming as a baby at the first Christmas. But it also looks forward to his second Advent. When Jesus ascended into heaven in full view of his disciples, God's messengers told them that "this same Jesus … will come back" (Acts 1 v 11).

There is much more in the New Testament about Jesus' return than there is about Christmas. You wouldn't think so if you take your Christianity from popular culture. But Jesus will come back—publicly, unmistakeably, in glory and great power. Indeed, he *must* come back. As the writer of the letter to the Hebrews explains, "Just as people are destined to die once, and after that to face judgment, so Christ was sacrificed once to take away the sins of many; and he will appear a second time, not to bear sin, but to bring salvation to those who are waiting for him" (Hebrews 9 v 27-28). Now *that* is a day worth waiting for.

These meditations will help you to reclaim the double edge to the season of Advent. As we reflect on the Jesus who came as a baby all those centuries ago, let us never forget that we are waiting, longing, yearning, praying for that great day when he will return. For the Jesus whom Luke reveals to us at the start of his Gospel is "this same Jesus" who will come back in glory. The more deeply we understand him in his first Advent, the more passionately we shall long for his return, when we shall see him face to face; and the more joyfully we will celebrate his arrival at the first Christmas.

LUKE 1 v 1-4

[1] Many have undertaken to draw up an
account of the things that have been fulfilled
among us, [2] just as they were handed down
to us by those who from the first were eye
witnesses and servants of the word. [3] With
this in mind, since I myself have carefully
investigated everything from the beginning,
I too decided to write an orderly account for
you, most excellent Theophilus, [4] so that you
may know the certainty of the things you have
been taught.

A REASSURING CERTAINTY

"Certainty" is a great word. Yet certainty is certainly hard to find.

In recent days I have come across reports of two general elections, in Sweden and Brazil, through different newsfeeds, newspapers or TV channels. It is astonishing what very different stories these sources tell, depending on the particular angle with which each wants to spin their account. Maybe you share my frustration. You want to know what actually happened, with fair reporting and balanced assessment, but somehow everyone has their own spin on things, and you flounder in a world of fake news and post-truth (as it has been called by the *Oxford English Dictionary*). If only, you say, I could find something really and certainly true.

But then, at other times we enjoy living in a fantasy world. There's long been an appeal to losing ourselves in a good fictional story. Now technology means we can even play a part in such a story, and walk around as an avatar in a virtual world, choosing what type of creature we are, what we wear, what powers we want to have, how we behave, what we say—and all without any real-world consequences. No wonder it's attractive!

And, to be honest, the Christmas season can feel a bit like that: a happy, cosy make-believe world of santas and elves and reindeer and *The Snowman* and *The Polar Express*—all enjoyed without even having to feel cold. Plenty of people think Christmas is a sugary fiction to make us feel better in the middle of winter—a form of extended escapism and "retail therapy".

But it's not. At least, the Bible's Christmas isn't. Before telling us the story, Luke carefully shows us that what he is about to say is TRUE. Really true—True with a capital "T". Lots of people have written accounts of it all. Luke calls these "the things that have been *fulfilled* among us" because everything he's going to say is a ful-filment—a filling full—of what we call the Old Testa-ment. These things didn't happen out of nowhere. The Old Testament has shadows and outlines of what would happen, and especially of *who* would come. The story Luke tells shows how Jesus fills those outlines full. Here we will find certainty.

The stories have come to Luke from "those who from the first were eye witnesses" (v 2). They were there; they saw, they heard, they touched these things. And they were "servants of the word"; that means they didn't make it up to suit themselves; the word was the master, and they were its servants—or perhaps we should say *his* servants. The apostle John writes about "that which was from the beginning, which we have heard, which we have seen with our eyes, which we have looked at and our hands have touched" (1 John 1 v 1). Here we will find certainty.

Luke has very "carefully investigated everything" right from "the beginning" (Luke 1 v 3). And now he has written an "orderly account" for a man called Theophilus (which means something like "friend of God"). The reason Luke has written is so that Theophilus—and now we too—can "know the certainty" about these things (v 4). Rock-solid reliable, True, certain.

Escapism is alright, so long as we know that's what it is. Two of my favourite Christmas movies are *Miracle on 34th Street* and *The Preacher's Wife*. They're wonderful. But they're not remotely true.

Jesus Christ is not like Santa Claus. One day each one of us will come face to face with truth, face to face with Jesus. When we die, or when Jesus returns, it will be no good trying to escape into a fictional world; it won't pass to say, "But I like to think..." this or that about God and about Jesus. That will be a great day, but perhaps also a frightening one. Luke tells us the truth now so that we can be ready to meet with truth then.

So ask yourself: What areas of my life are so painful that I take refuge in fantasy? What doubts cloud my contentment in the truth of Jesus? Meditate today on the sureness of the truth as it is in Christ. Thank God that his message is certain, solid, reliable, true. You can rest your life on it. How wonderful to find certainty!

SING

Tell me the old, old story
Of unseen things above,
Of Jesus and his glory,
Of Jesus and his love:
Tell me the story simply,
As to a little child,
For I am weak and weary,
And helpless and defiled.

(Katherine Hankey, 1834-1911)

PRAY

Blessed Lord, who has caused all the Bible to be written for our learning, we thank you that the story we hear from Luke is true and safe and secure, and we can rest our lives and our eternal destinies upon the message we hear in it. Grant that, as we meditate quietly on this old, old story, our hearts may be comforted by the solid certainty that these things are true. May we know in some fresh way this Advent the comfort of your holy word, and embrace and hold it fast in our hearts and minds. Through Jesus Christ our Lord, Amen.

JOURNAL

_____

_____

_____

_____

_____

_____

_____

_____

_____

_____

_____

_____

_____

_____

_____

_____

_____

_____

LUKE 1 v 5-7

⁵ In the time of Herod king of Judea there was a priest named Zechariah, who belonged to the priestly division of Abijah; his wife Elizabeth was also a descendant of Aaron. ⁶ Both of them were righteous in the sight of God, observing all the Lord's commands and decrees blamelessly. ⁷ But they were childless because Elizabeth was not able to conceive, and they were both very old.

A POIGNANT HOPE

"**B**ut they were childless." Before we speed on to the rest of the story, let's quietly pause at these sad words. For some, to do so will cause terrible personal pain. And all of us, perhaps, will feel keenly the sorrow of those whom we love and who are childless: those who have never married, but who would love to have married; others who are married, but for whom the birth of a child has never been given by God. Childless.

It is, as one childless couple has said, "that strange grief which has no focus for its tears and no object for its love". There is no anniversary of childlessness on which friends might send a card of condolence, no grave to visit and remember, no photograph or name or memory of the child who never came. It is just an emptiness, a not-ness, a joy that didn't come, a hope for ever dashed.

Zechariah and Elizabeth were married. They hoped and prayed for a child, for they valued highly such a wonderful gift of God. But the child never came. The months went by, but there was no conception. Gradually the biological clock ticked on to the years when it seemed unlikely to happen, and finally into that stage of life when it was most definitely not going to happen. Many tears, much quiet grieving. And no hope. Childless.

Yet however painful it might be to pause here in the story, it is important to do so. For it will deepen our grasp of the nature and the wonder of the gospel of the Lord Jesus. And that depth of wonder will more than compensate for the tears we may shed.

Childlessness is a poignant motif in the story of the Bible. Abraham and Sarah are childless—until Isaac is given; Isaac and Rebecca are childless—until Esau and Jacob are born; Jacob and Rachel are childless—until Joseph is given; and there were others. And now Zechariah and Elizabeth, this godly priest and his pious wife, are added to the list.

It is clear that for none of these couples was their childlessness a punishment from God for their sin. And yet, after her son, John, is conceived, Elizabeth describes her former childlessness as a "disgrace" among her people: "'The Lord has done this for me,' she said. 'In these days he has shown his favour and taken away my disgrace among the people'" (1 v 25).

Some would have considered Elizabeth's childlessness to be a disgrace because they thought it was a punishment from God for her sin. (The friends who come to "comfort" the Old Testament character Job in his misery think like this.) Such people would have been wrong. Luke describes Zechariah and Elizabeth in glowing terms as profoundly righteous people who keep the law of God because they believe all the promises of God.

And yet there is a sense in which their childlessness is a "dis-grace"; for it is a peculiarly vivid example of the misery of living in a world under sin and the righteous judgment of God. Every sickness, every sadness, every disability is—in this sense—visible evidence that we live in a world under the righteous judgement of God. No doubt there are marks in your life at the moment that show you too are living in a world under judgment; we are all marked in some way with what Elizabeth calls "disgrace".

And therefore—and this is the wonderful significance of what happens—the removal of this "disgrace" is a sign of the kindness and mercy of God, as "dis-grace" is swept away by grace. Again and again in the Bible story this is what the birth of an unexpected child means—from Isaac onwards. It is a sign of the gospel. A world with no new children would be a sad and forever ageing world, a world without hope. Every child is a sign of hope for the future, a bundle of unknown possibilities, a sign of what we call God's "common grace"—his kindness to all humankind. And this unexpected child, John the Baptist, is a sign not just of God's common grace to all, but specifically of God's particular kindness in what he is about to do in the gospel of Jesus.

The conception and birth of John the Baptist does not mean that every yearning of a childless couple will issue in a happy birth. Far from it. There have always been, and will be to the end of time, godly, prayerful couples who long for children and are not given them. None of us can know, when we get married, whether or not God will grant us this precious gift.

But we can all know that the conception and birth of John the Baptist points forward to a much greater gift. The particularly painful "dis-grace" experienced by Elizabeth and Zechariah is vividly replaced by a gift of grace. That boy will be the herald of a deeper and more wonderful grace. So whether your present experience is of sadness or joy, use today quietly to pin your hopes not upon a change in your circumstances but upon the great hope for the future to which this baby, John the Baptist, points so clearly. Think about your marks of "disgrace"; thank God that in Christ they are not a punishment for your personal sins; and rejoice that when Jesus returns, every one of those painful marks will be taken away.

SING

> *Hark, the glad sound! The Saviour comes,*
> *The Saviour promised long;*
> *Let ev'ry heart prepare a throne,*
> *And every voice a song.*
>
> *He comes the broken heart to bind,*
> *The bleeding soul to cure;*
> *And with the treasures of his grace*
> *To enrich the humble poor.*
>
> *(Philip Doddridge, 1702-1751)*

PRAY

God our heavenly Father, as we grieve for the miseries of this world, and especially as we weep with those who weep in childlessness, we thank you that by the birth of John the Baptist you gave us a herald of hope: that in the new heavens and new earth all who belong to Christ will rejoice in the overwhelming goodness that will fulfil and exceed all our godly longings. Even in the midst of our tears, give us thankful hearts, we pray. For Jesus' sake, Amen.

JOURNAL

_____

_____

_____

_____

_____

_____

_____

_____

_____

_____

_____

_____

LUKE 1 v 8-17

8 Once when Zechariah's division was on duty and he was serving as priest before God, 9 he was chosen by lot, according to the custom of the priesthood, to go into the temple of the Lord and burn incense. 10 And when the time for the burning of incense came, all the assembled worshippers were praying outside.

11 Then an angel of the Lord appeared to Zechariah ... 13 "Do not be afraid, Zechariah; your prayer has been heard. Your wife Elizabeth will bear you a son, and you are to call him John. 14 He will be a joy and delight to you, and many will rejoice because of his birth, 15 for he will be great in the sight of the Lord. He is never to take wine or other fermented drink, and he will be filled with the Holy Spirit even before he is born. 16 He will bring back many of the people of Israel to the Lord their God. 17 And he will go on before the Lord, in the spirit and power of Elijah, to turn the hearts of the parents to their children and the disobedient to the wisdom of the righteous—to make ready a people prepared for the Lord."

3
COMING HOME

Many of us will go home for Christmas. Perhaps we live far away, where we work or study. But at Christmas we go home. And for so many families, when a son or daughter comes home, it is a cause for great joy. There will be hugs and exclamations: "How lovely to have you home again!" Special food will be served, presents lovingly wrapped will be opened, there will be cheerful chatter and much happiness. It is not always like that—and Christmas is a sad time for too many—but when things are well, there is something wonderful about coming home. An exuberant mother may even want to rush out and give a present to the bus driver who has brought her child home!

John the Baptist is, in a way, like that bus driver; he is going to be a man who brings people home. What the angel says is full of joy. John will be "a joy and delight" to his parents (v 14), for they are godly parents and, as they watch their child grow, they will delight to see his loyal love for God. They will remember their long wait for a child and thank God day after day for giving them such a son. But not only will John be "a joy and delight to you" (his parents); others too will be happy, for "many will rejoice because of his birth". Here is a son who will bring overflowing joy to men and women throughout the land. Why? It's not just that everybody is happy that this long-childless couple now have a fine strong son. It is far deeper than that.

He won't drink wine, perhaps as an outward sign of his special dedication to God. Even while he is grow-ing in Elizabeth's womb, he will be "filled with the Holy Spirit" (v 15). This baby boy is set apart for a holy life, a life of beautiful distinctiveness, of moral purity, of loving dedication to God, from even before he is born. The Spirit of God, the third Person of the Trinity, God himself, will live and breathe in John's heart.

So what will happen when God the Holy Spirit lives and breathes through this man? He will do what God loves to do. God loves to bring people home; so this Spirit-filled man will bring people home. He will "bring back many of the people of Israel to the Lord their God" (v 16). That is why there will be such joy. All over the land, men and women who are far from God, not trust-ing him, will come back in repentance and faith. And they will thank God for John the Baptist, who brought them home. He will be like the great Old Testament prophet Elijah, who called the people to repentance (1 Kings 18).

And it's not just that John will bring people back home to God. He will also bring them home to one another. The "hearts of the parents" and "their children" may be shorthand for whole generations: a brief way of speaking of all kinds of painful alienation (v 17). When we are in the far country, a long way from God, we put up many barriers between ourselves—we fall out with children or parents, we hate other races, we mistreat women, we resent those we don't get on with in the workplace. And so John will turn hearts back to God and to one another. Marriages will be saved and families put back together. No wonder there will be joy! Think about relationship pains in your life or family. How much they hurt! Ask God to do that "bringing home" work in you and others.

Best of all, John will "make ready a people prepared for the Lord", prepared for God himself to come and rescue them. John is not just the bringing-home prophet; he is the getting-ready-for-God prophet. When we read on in Luke's Gospel, we find that the men and women who came home to God when John preached were precisely the people who were ready to welcome God's King (Luke 7 v 29-30).

Meditate today on just how joyous it is to repent: to turn from living for yourself, to turn from your sinful self-centredness, and to come home to the God who welcomes you. This is the God who sent John the Baptist to bring people home. It is good to look forward to happy homecomings at this time of year. But when you find yourself thinking about those moments—relishing the anticipation of that sweet hello, or dreading the tension of that awkward encounter—remember the God who stands to welcome you home. The joy of that homecoming to God is far better even than the happiest Christmas homecoming.

☾SING

> *Come let us sing of a wonderful love,*
> *Tender and true,*
> *Out of the heart of the Father above,*
> *Streaming to me and to you:*
> *Wonderful love*
> *Dwells in the heart of the Father above.*
>
> *Jesus is seeking the wanderers yet;*
> *Why do they roam?*
> *Love only waits to forgive and forget;*
> *Home! Weary wanderer, home!*
> *Wonderful love*
> *Dwells in the heart of the Father above.*
>
> *(Gerhard Tersteegen, 1697-1769)*

☽PRAY

Almighty God, who sent your servant John the Baptist to call people to repentance and to prepare the way for the Lord Jesus, who came to seek and to save the lost: grant that, as we remember John's birth with joy, we too may turn to you with all our hearts and wait joyfully for that day when the Lord Jesus will return to rescue all who are waiting for him. For Jesus' sake, Amen.

JOURNAL

_____

_____

_____

_____

_____

_____

_____

_____

_____

_____

_____

_____

_____

_____

_____

_____

_____

_____

_____

_____

LUKE 1 v 18-25

[18] Zechariah asked the angel, "How can I be sure of this? I am an old man and my wife is well on in years."

[19] The angel said to him, "I am Gabriel. I stand in the presence of God, and I have been sent to speak to you and to tell you this good news. [20] And now you will be silent and not able to speak until the day this happens, because you did not believe my words, which will come true at their appointed time."

[21] Meanwhile, the people were waiting for Zechariah and wondering why he stayed so long in the temple. [22] When he came out, he could not speak to them. They realised he had seen a vision in the temple, for he kept making signs to them but remained unable to speak.

[23] When his time of service was completed, he returned home. [24] After this his wife Elizabeth became pregnant and for five months remained in seclusion. [25] "The Lord has done this for me," she said. "In these days he has shown his favour and taken away my disgrace among the people."

RESTING ON A WORD

F aith is a strange thing. Somehow it is possible to believe and not to believe, and all at the same time. Luke tells us that Zechariah and his wife, Elizabeth, were "righteous in the sight of God, observing all the Lord's commands and decrees blamelessly" (v 6). That doesn't mean that they were legalists, trying to get right with God by keeping the law. Not at all! You could never be "righteous" before God like that; righteousness is always by faith, as Abraham learned (Genesis 15 v 6). No, it means they were believers. They kept the law because they believed the promises which were embedded throughout the Old Testament law. Despite the misery of the world and the sadnesses of the people of God, they believed that one day God would send a Messiah, a Saviour, and fulfil all his promises.

And Zechariah and Elizabeth lived their law-keeping, believing lives "blamelessly". That doesn't mean sinlessly.

It means they were genuine; it means that what you saw outwardly in Zechariah and Elizabeth fitted with what they were inwardly. They weren't hypocrites; they had integrity; they lived with a clear conscience; they were true believers. All down the Old Testament centuries there were "blameless" believers like this couple. Sometimes the Bible calls them a "remnant", because the majority of the Israelites were not like this. Perhaps one of the earliest such believers was Job, who is three times described as "blameless" (Job 1 v 1; 1 v 8; 2 v 3).

What a terrific couple Zechariah and Elizabeth were! I would love to have met them, as they went on and on believing, through the sadness of childlessness, right into old age. And yet, when Gabriel the angel speaks to Zechariah as a messenger from God, Zechariah does not believe him (Luke 1 v 18). He is a believer, and yet an unbeliever. He doesn't believe Gabriel for the same reason we might find faith difficult today: the evidence of his senses. He knows that he is an old man; every cell in his body, every muscle, every ache, every weary groan tells him he is an old man. He knows he is past being a father. And he knows that Elizabeth is "well on in years" (a nice, gracious way of saying she is an old lady, well past her child-bearing years). There is lots of simple, tangible, visible evidence of this. All their senses tell them they are too old to have a baby.

What Zechariah hears is—in a manner of speaking— the supernatural gospel. There is a living God who is the Creator and source of all life, including especially the procreation of a new human life. And this living God speaks. We find angels puzzling in our sceptical and rather arrogant culture; but they simply mean that God speaks, and sometimes he does so through supernatural messengers (which is what "angel" means). Gabriel stands in the presence of God; he is a senior member of God's court. And God has sent him "to tell you this good news" (v 19—literally, "to evangelise you").

So Zechariah has to choose. On the one hand he has the clear evidence of all his senses; on the other he hears a word of good news, a gospel, from a messenger of God. It is not at all surprising that he hesitates: "How can I be sure?" That question has echoed down the centuries. We hear this gospel word, this promise; but we look at our life and the world, and we wonder how we can be sure that this word is true. Perhaps there is some teaching in God's word that makes you wonder, "How can I be sure?"

And so Zechariah is struck dumb for a time. This is not so much a punishment as necessary discipline. He is a priest, with responsibilities for teaching the people God's word. But now he needs a period when he can listen, or think quietly about what he has heard, until he sees the evidence that the word was true (which he most certainly will).

The "gospel" that Zechariah hears is just a trailer for the full gospel that is to follow. It is amazing, and it is not surprising that Zechariah struggles to believe it; but the news that follows will be infinitely more wonderful. We too hear this full gospel, not usually by a supernatural vision of an angel but by the reliable words now recorded for us in our Bibles. These words come from the presence of God, who has sent his messengers—the prophets and the apostles—to tell us this good news.

Perhaps you, like Zechariah, find that you believe and do not really believe, all at the same time. I doubt if you will literally be struck dumb. But there may be a need for us also to talk less and listen more: to give ourselves time and space to meditate on the gospel of the Lord Jesus, which Zechariah's son would herald. It is an amazing gospel that brings life to the dead, just as—in this trailer—it brought the new life of a baby to a man and a woman who were as good as dead. You will grow in confidence as you take time to thank God for the wonderful life-giving gospel.

SING

> *Here, Lord, relying on thy Word,*
> *I claim thy promise true,*
> *That whosoe'er receiveth thee*
> *At once is born anew.*
> > *E.H. Gladstone Sargent (1887-1973)*

PRAY

God our Father, who has promised new life to those who have no hope, as you promised a son to this old couple who were beyond hoping: grant us grace to listen, to trust, and to set our hopes on the gospel you speak to us, that we may live by faith and not by sight. For Jesus' sake, Amen.

JOURNAL

_____
_____
_____
_____
_____
_____
_____
_____
_____
_____
_____
_____
_____
_____
_____
_____
_____
_____
_____
_____
_____
_____

LUKE 1 v 26-33

²⁶ In the sixth month of Elizabeth's pregnancy, God sent the angel Gabriel to Nazareth, a town in Galilee, ²⁷ to a virgin pledged to be married to a man named Joseph, a descendant of David. The virgin's name was Mary. ²⁸ The angel went to her and said, "Greetings, you who are highly favoured! The Lord is with you."

²⁹ Mary was greatly troubled at his words and wondered what kind of greeting this might be. ³⁰ But the angel said to her, "Do not be afraid, Mary, you have found favour with God. ³¹ You will conceive and give birth to a son, and you are to call him Jesus. ³² He will be great and will be called the Son of the Most High. The Lord God will give him the throne of his father David, ³³ and he will reign over Jacob's descendants for ever; his kingdom will never end."

GOOD GOVERNMENT
AT LAST

We're five days into Luke's Gospel, and you may by now be wondering when Jesus is going to get a mention. After all, we know Christmas is not about Santa Claus or reindeer or fairy lights or presents; it's about Jesus. So why haven't we heard about him yet? Answer: we need the "warm up" so that we can understand Jesus when we are told about him.

One of the (many) reasons I love the Bible is the way God speaks to us in language we can understand. If a philosopher wanted to introduce Jesus, we might be left swimming around in long words. But not so with Luke's introduction. The story of Zechariah and Elizabeth sends us scurrying back to read the Old Testament. Zechariah is a priest in the temple. The conception of their child echoes other Old Testament miracle-babies from Isaac onwards. So, as readers, our minds are thinking Old Testament.

And now, as the angel Gabriel goes on his second mission, to visit Mary, everything he says about Jesus is in Old Testament language. He tells Mary four simple and wonderful things about her soon-to-be-conceived baby boy.

First, Mary's son will be a *king*. That's all about David. Her fiancé, Joseph, is "a descendant of David" (v 27); Joseph will be the legal (adoptive) father of the boy, so the boy will be counted in law as descended from David. God will give the boy "the throne of his father David" (v 32). So we scurry back to 2 Samuel 7, where we learn of God's amazing promises to David—pledges that won't be fulfilled until Jesus reigns. One day there'll be a perfect King. David was a great king, but far from perfect (think of Uriah and Bathsheba in 2 Samuel 11). But one day there will be a perfect King.

Second, Mary's boy will "be called the *Son*" of God (Luke 4 v 32). David and his dynasty were called "sons" of God (see Psalm 2); but Mary's boy will have a real, deep eternal and intimate relationship with God the Father. He will make God the Father known. He will love God the Father, and God the Father will love him, with an unbreakable love. All our longings for intimacy, security and love will be fulfilled through this boy, this Son. For the first time in human history, somebody will love God with heart, mind, soul and strength. When our human rulers govern, mostly they think too much about themselves; but this Ruler will govern in loving loyalty to God his Father. He will not puff himself up; he will not grab at privileges or use corruption to get his way. No, he will be the first ruler in human history to love God perfectly.

Third, Mary's son will be entrusted with *very great power*. He will be "the Son of the Most High" (Luke 1 v 32); the "Most High" is a very old title for the all-powerful God. He governs every thing in every place. This new King "will reign over Jacob's descendants" (v 33, which means the believing Jews, and all the Gentiles who believe in the Messiah and are grafted in to the people of God). We worry when a human ruler gets too much power. That's why our wisest systems of government have checks and balances, so that nobody wields absolute power. We can't trust them to. Absolute power corrupts absolutely. But for this King, absolute power is just what we want him to have, for he will use it for perfect justice.

Fourth, this boy's reign will *never end*. Our problem is that bad governments often go on too long, and good governments don't last. But for this King, "his kingdom will never end" (v 33). When Jesus returns to earth, Mary's boy will be seen as the ruler of the new creation for all eternity. We need not worry that he will be toppled, or die, or abuse his power. For his will be the perfect reign that the whole creation has longed for ever since Adam messed up his job of ruling the world.

It's not difficult to understand what Gabriel says to Mary—her son will be a King who fulfils the promises to David; a King in a beautiful relationship as the Son of God the Father; a King with absolute power, who will never abuse that power; and a King whose reign will never end. No, it's not hard to understand. But sometimes it's hard to take in the scope of just how wonderful it is.

Look at today's news headlines. What frustrates or saddens you about your government, or the senior management in your workplace? Where is corruption, self-interest or just plain attention-seeking evident, and ugly in its effects? Meditate on that; but then turn your thoughts to rejoice in Jesus the King, and to look forward and long for his return, when he will enter fully into his kingdom, and the will of God will finally be done on earth in the same way that it is done in heaven.

SING

> *I cannot tell how all the lands shall worship,*
> *When at his bidding every storm is stilled,*
> *Or who can say how great the jubilation*
> *When all our hearts with love for him are filled.*
> *But this I know, the skies will sound his praises,*
> *Ten thousand thousand human voices sing,*
> *And earth to heaven,*
> *and heaven to earth, will answer,*
> *"At last the Saviour, Saviour of the world,*
> *is King!"*
>
> (William Young Fullerton, 1857-1932)

PRAY

Father God, thank you that Jesus your Son is the perfect King in David's line. We praise you that he will wield your almighty power. We rejoice that he loves you as your loyal Son. We are comforted that his reign will never end. As we look beyond Christmas to that future day, we say in our hearts at this Advent time, "Come, Lord Jesus!" Amen.

JOURNAL

LUKE 1 v 26-27, 34-35

[26] In the sixth month of Elizabeth's pregnancy, God sent the angel Gabriel to Nazareth, a town in Galilee, [27] to a virgin pledged to be married …

[34] "How will this be," Mary asked the angel, "since I am a virgin?"

[35] The angel answered, "The Holy Spirit will come on you, and the power of the Most High will overshadow you. So the holy one to be born will be called the Son of God."

CONCEIVED OF A VIRGIN

Today we meditate on the virgin birth of Jesus. Or, to be more accurate, the virgin conception of Jesus, which began the pregnancy of his virgin mother.

The Bible is very clear that Mary conceived the boy Jesus before she had slept with any man. She was engaged to Joseph but had not slept with him (v 27); she would not sleep with him until after they were married and Jesus was born (Matthew 1 v 25). She was a godly young woman; Joseph was a righteous man. They lived in a culture that valued virginity before marriage, in a way that is foreign to our society but right and beautiful. They knew as well as we do that babies are not conceived except by the natural process of human procreation.

So, when Gabriel tells Mary that she will conceive a baby, she is very surprised. Very, very surprised. "How will this be ... since I am a virgin?" (Luke 1 v 34).

The virgin conception of the Lord Jesus is both wonderful and meaningful; it points us to at least three facets of the incarnation. First, this miracle makes it clear that the sending of Jesus was entirely the sovereign work of God himself. The astonishing births of Isaac, Jacob and Esau, and then others in the Old Testament all the way down to John the Baptist, at least involved both a father and mother who wanted a child and—as we put it—were "trying for a baby". They were sleeping together and praying that conception would ensue. But this most astonishing conception of them all involves no human desire or intention or involvement; God simply does this miracle by his own sovereign decision in the womb of the very surprised Mary (and to the surprise of the uninvolved Joseph).

The apostle John writes that Christians are given "the right to become children of God—children born [spiritually] not of natural descent, nor of human decision or a husband's will"; instead we are "born of God" (John 1 v 12-13). What becomes true of us spiritually by new birth (entirely the decision and initiative of God) echoes what was true of the Lord Jesus' supernatural conception: no human desire or husband's will was involved. No human beings did anything to help God send Jesus; God decided to do it, and he did it. There is no room for spiritual smugness on our part.

Second—and this follows from the first point—the virgin conception of Jesus proves to us that God did not adopt Jesus as his Son. Sometimes people suggest that Jesus was a remarkable man, and so God decided to adopt him as his Son, perhaps at his baptism or at his birth. But the virgin conception means that from the very first moment of his human existence, Jesus was (and had always been) the Son of God. Indeed, in that instant the One who had been God the Son from all eternity took upon himself a human nature: "the Word became flesh" (John 1 v 14). There was no time in Jesus' human life when he was anything other than the eternal Son of God made flesh.

This moment—this hidden, unwitnessed instant in the womb of the virgin Mary—was the most astonishing miracle in all of human history. The virgin conception of Jesus points, thirdly, to the mystery that this boy was at the same time both fully human—inheriting a fully human nature from Mary—and also fully divine. He was, as theologians later described it, one undivided person possessed of two natures: the divine nature he had possessed from all eternity and the human nature he was given from Mary. In some astonishing way that we can never completely describe or analyse, Jesus Christ was, and is, fully man and fully God. He is fully human, and yet without the taint and defilement of the sinful, spoiled nature that each of us inherits from our father and mother.

This matters. It means that, standing in heaven now at the right hand of the Father, there is a perfect high priest who is able "to feel sympathy for our weaknesses", who "has been tempted in every way, just as we are—yet he did not sin" (Hebrews 4 v 15). Jesus understands that loss of temper with your housemate, that selfish decision for your own comfort over serving others, that lustful or covetous thought. He knows. And yet he was without sin; and so he can save you out of it all.

No wonder Christians down the ages have stood in awe and wonder as they—and now we—have contemplated the miracle of Jesus Christ, the Son of God made flesh.

SING

> *God of God, Light of Light,*
> *Lo, he abhors not the virgin's womb;*
> *Very God, begotten, not created;*
> *O come, let us adore him,*
> *O come, let us adore him,*
> *O come, let us adore him, Christ the Lord.*
> *(Attributed to John Francis Wage, 1711-1786)*

PRAY

"Almighty God, who hast given us thy only begotten Son to take our nature upon him, and as at this time to be born of a pure virgin; grant that we being regenerate, and made thy children by adoption and grace, may daily be renewed by thy holy Spirit; through the same our Lord Jesus Christ, who liveth and reigneth with thee and the same Spirit ever, one God, world without end. Amen." (Collect for Christmas Day from the Book of Common Prayer)

JOURNAL

_____

_____

_____

_____

_____

_____

_____

_____

_____

_____

_____

_____

_____

_____

_____

_____

_____

_____

_____

_____

LUKE 1 v 34-35

[34] "How will this be," Mary asked the angel, "since I am a virgin?" [35] The angel answered, "The Holy Spirit will come on you, and the power of the Most High will overshadow you. So the holy one to be born will be called the Son of God."

A POWERFUL
OVERSHADOWING

*C*hristmas is a busy time for many of us. Perhaps you've started sighing over the state of your to-do list: the packed schedule of social engagements and church events to get through between now and the new year. Every December is the same.

Why do we do it to ourselves? I think, in part, it's this: being busy makes us feel important.

Luke 1 v 35 describes what is perhaps the most wonderful moment in all of human history. Yet it is a completely hidden moment. Meanwhile the busy men and women who thought they mattered—the really important and powerful people, like the Roman emperor and those around him—went about their pressured and so, so important lives completely unaware. They would not have had the faintest idea that somewhere on the distant margins of their empire, something was happening that would change the world for ever.

Most of what we think about at Christmas is of the utmost triviality. Christmas is about tinsel and all things twinkly and superficial. This moment in Luke's Gospel is like none of those things. In answer to Mary's astonished question, Gabriel says that "the Holy Spirit will come on [her]" (v 35)—God the Holy Spirit, the third Person of the Holy Trinity, the One who, along with the Father and the Son, is fully God and has been from all eternity. But what does that mean? Gabriel goes on: "... and the power of the Most High will overshadow you". The Most High means the Holy Spirit here, for the Holy Spirit is—in all his divine fullness—the Most High God (just as the Father is the Most High God and the Son is the Most High God). So Gabriel is not telling Mary that two things will happen; he is describing one thing in two ways.

But look at that word "overshadow". It translates a very unusual word in the Scriptures. At the end of the book of Exodus, Moses cannot enter the tent of meeting because "the glory of the LORD filled the tabernacle" and the cloud of God's glory had "settled" on it (the same word as "overshadow", Exodus 40 v 34-35). In Psalm 91, God "will cover" (same word) his Messiah with his feathers, so that under God's wings the Messiah will find refuge (Psalm 91 v 4). At the transfiguration of Jesus, the bright glory cloud "covered" him and his disciples (same word, Mark 9 v 7). It's a word that speaks of the personal presence of God on earth to bring protection to his Messiah and all who belong to him. God the Holy Spirit overshadows Mary and creates in her womb a body, a fully human body, for the Son of God to take upon himself. Here, in this hidden moment, with no spectators, no ultrasound scans, no fanfare, the eternal Spirit of God creates a body for the eternal Son of God to take upon himself our nature, that he may save us.

Although different words are used in Genesis 1, the imagery reminds us of the Spirit "hovering" over the shapeless waters to create the world; but now he hovers over the womb of the virgin to begin the new creation. All down Old Testament history there were hints that one day God himself would dwell on earth. The tabernacle and later the temple were the clearest of those foreshadowings. At rare and special times, the glory cloud enveloped, covered, settled, overshadowed the tabernacle and the temple. God himself dwelt on earth. But now, in the womb of Mary, as the Holy Spirit overshadows her, God himself comes in the reality of human flesh and blood to dwell on earth.

The letter to the Hebrews says that Christ speaks these words (quoting from the Greek translation of Psalm 40): "A body you prepared for me" (Hebrews 10 v 5). This is the miracle on which we meditate today. The Holy Spirit prepares a body for God the Son. God the Son takes upon himself that body—not just the flesh and bones but the full humanness of a human mind, human emotions, a human will, a human spirit—in order to do the will of the Father and rescue us. This is true humility. Christ took our human nature; why then do we need to feel important? If we grasp his astonishing humility, we can slow down our frenetic activity; we can rest our weary bodies because he took one such mortal body himself. That body, now glorified in resurrection power, he still indwells and will do for all eternity.

SING

> Behold, the great Creator makes
> Himself a house of clay;
> A robe of human form he takes
> For ever from this day.

> This wonder all the world amazed
> And shook the starry frame;
> The hosts of heaven stood and gazed,
> Then blessed the Saviour's name.
>
> *(Thomas Pestel, 1584-1659)*

PRAY

"Merciful and most loving God, by whose will and bountiful gift Jesus Christ our Lord humbled himself that he might exalt humankind; and became flesh that he might restore in us the most celestial image; and was born of the virgin that he might uplift the lowly: grant unto us the inheritance of the meek, perfect us in thy likeness, and bring us at last to rejoice in beholding thy beauty, and with all thy saints to glorify thy grace; through the same Jesus Christ our Lord, Amen." (Gallican Sacramentary)

JOURNAL

_____

_____

_____

_____

_____

_____

_____

_____

_____

_____

_____

_____

_____

_____

_____

_____

_____

_____

_____

_____

_____

_____

_____

_____

_____

LUKE 1 v 34-38

[34] "How will this be," Mary asked the angel, "since I am a virgin?"

[35] The angel answered, "The Holy Spirit will come on you, and the power of the Most High will overshadow you. So the holy one to be born will be called the Son of God. [36] Even Elizabeth your relative is going to have a child in her old age, and she who was said to be unable to conceive is in her sixth month. [37] For no word from God will ever fail."

[38] "I am the Lord's servant," Mary answered. "May your word to me be fulfilled." Then the angel left her.

8 TRUE FAITH

Almost as astonishing as the angel's message is the fact that Mary believes him! Put yourself in the shoes of a young, unmarried girl. You see an angel. (Well, you *think* you see an angel.) And you hear the angel telling you... well, some pretty amazing things. (Or you *think* you hear him.) So what do you say to yourself? I can think of plenty of ways to get around it: "I ate something odd last night and had a strange hallucination." "My imagination has been over-stimulated." "Dreams are so odd." However you explain it, I think we can agree that we would not have done what Mary did: which was to take the angel's words at face value. It is extraordinary. She doesn't ask *whether* it will happen; she asks *how* it will happen.

To which the answer—which no doubt puzzled her greatly—is that the Holy Spirit will come upon her; and therefore her child will be "the Son of God" (v 35). All three Persons of the holy Trinity will be involved in this miracle: the Father, who sent the Son; the Son, who took flesh; and the Holy Spirit, by whose agency the Son was conceived in Mary's womb.

Mary's faith is a great miracle, given to her by God. Think for a moment about the contrast with Zechariah. Zechariah was a senior man; Mary is a junior woman. Zechariah was a priest in the temple; he was surrounded by the visible signs of the living God and his covenant with his people. Day after day, he was reminded of the Scriptures and the reality of the all-powerful God. He worked at the heart of Israel's life. But Mary lives in the north, in the despised region of Galilee, in an utterly insignificant village called Nazareth; it is the kind of place about which people sneer, "Can anything good come from *there*?" (John 1 v 46). Mary is a nobody from nowhere that matters; Zechariah was a somebody from somewhere that counted. And yet, in a most wonderful twist, Mary demonstrates simple faith where Zechariah struggled. We saw that Zechariah was a godly man; he was a believer; he was not a hypocrite or a legalist. But he struggled to believe that he and his wife, elderly as they were, could conceive a baby. Mary hears the word of God and believes something even more astonishing: that she, a virgin, will conceive!

Mary's example helps us to reflect on the nature of true faith. First, we see that faith is based on words. God speaks words to Mary through the angel. The angel tells her that "no word from God will ever fail" (Luke 1 v 37). Mary believes what God speaks. She asks that his "word to me be fulfilled" (v 38). Faith is by its very nature not the same as sight. We live, as Mary had to live, by faith and not by sight. She needed to trust the words of God. The Bible teaches us not to expect, in the normal Christian life, the kind of angelic appearance that Mary experienced. But we are given, in the Bible, just the same reliable words—words that will never fail. Faith means believing the words God has spoken to us, just as for Mary it meant believing the words spoken to her.

But notice, also, that God in his kindness does give Mary some evidence to reassure her. Mary has already trusted the words. But in his answer to the question, "How?" the angel tells Mary that her elderly cousin Elizabeth, whom everybody thought was much too old ever to have a child, is now almost six months pregnant. That doesn't prove to Mary that she, a virgin, will conceive. But it is evidence that there is a living God. It reassures Mary that the God in whom she trusts is doing wonderful things in the world already. In a similar way, God has given us evidence of his power to do wonderful deeds. The Bible is full of such evidence, and the changed lives of men and women around us are powerful evidence that God is real and true. Take a moment to think about one or two people in your church in whom you have seen God especially at work in this past year. This evidence of God at work helps us to trust his words, as it no doubt helped Mary.

And trusting God's word will mean we obey God's word. Faith and obedience are intimately connected. Believing, for Mary, meant much more than an intellectual assent to the angel's words. When Mary prays, "May your word to me be fulfilled", she is offering herself to God—her womb, her body, her whole vulnerable person—in loving submission and trusting obedience. This is true faith. In his letter to the Romans, Paul calls it "the obedience that comes from faith" (Romans 1 v 5; 16 v 26). To believe is to obey, and to obey from a heart of trust is to believe. Spend a moment examining your heart. Is there a particular way in which real faith in your heart will show itself in some new obedience to God?

Today let us wonder at the radiant beauty of Mary's faith, and pray that God will give us a faith like hers.

SING

Lord, thy word abideth,
And our footsteps guideth;
Who its truth believeth
Light and joy receiveth.

Who can tell the pleasure,
Who recount the treasure,
By thy word imparted
To the simple-hearted?

(H.W. Baker, 1821-1877)

PRAY

God our Father, who gave to the virgin Mary the faith to believe the word of the angel, grant to us that we too may trust that no word from you will ever fail, and that what you have given us in Jesus our Lord is trustworthy and true for this life and for eternity. We ask it for Jesus' sake. Amen.

JOURNAL

_____

_____

_____

_____

_____

_____

_____

_____

_____

_____

_____

_____

_____

_____

_____

_____

LUKE 1 v 39-45

39 At that time Mary got ready and hurried to a town in the hill country of Judea, 40 where she entered Zechariah's home and greeted Elizabeth. 41 When Elizabeth heard Mary's greeting, the baby leaped in her womb, and Elizabeth was filled with the Holy Spirit. 42 In a loud voice she exclaimed: "Blessed are you among women, and blessed is the child you will bear! 43 But why am I so favoured, that the mother of my Lord should come to me? 44 As soon as the sound of your greeting reached my ears, the baby in my womb leaped for joy. 45 Blessed is she who has believed that the Lord would fulfil his promises to her!"

9 JUMPING FOR JOY

When a mother feels a baby move in the womb, it is a very exciting moment. Of course, she already knew the little one was there. And nowadays she has probably seen astonishingly detailed ultrasound scans, and perhaps even shared them on social media. But when the little boy or girl kicks, or punches, or jumps in the womb, it's a great day. They—quite literally—make their presence felt. (Indeed, I know one mother whose baby boy kicked so hard that he cracked one of her ribs!)

Today we think about perhaps the most extraordinary "baby in the womb" moment in history and what it means. When the angel tells Mary that her elderly relative is in mid-pregnancy (v 36), she hurries over to see her. Imagine her, in your mind's eye, as she comes into the home and greets Elizabeth. Nothing surprising so far. But now it becomes clear that it's all the other way around. It's not so much Mary greeting Elizabeth as Elizabeth's baby greeting Mary's baby! It's the nearest we get to a play date in the womb!

The baby John the Baptist leaps in Elizabeth's womb so dramatically, so suddenly, so joyfully, at just the moment when Mary enters, that the world must be told of this moment through the pages of Scripture. This incident is not a coincidence (as if he "just happened" to move then); no, this is because John the Baptist senses who has just arrived. Elizabeth is filled with the Holy Spirit (who is active at every moment of these dramas). She knows what it means: "Blessed are you among women, and blessed is the child you will bear!" (v 42). We don't know if Mary has managed to send a message to Elizabeth to tell her that she is pregnant and what the angel said. I suspect not. But Elizabeth knows; the Holy Spirit tells her—and not only that Mary is pregnant but who her baby is.

Elizabeth greets Mary as "the mother of my Lord" (v 43), which is a most surprising way to speak to a young relative. And yet it is true. And—to show us how important it is—we hear again, from Elizabeth's lips, that at the very moment when Mary said "hello", Elizabeth's baby leaped in her womb "for joy". Joy bubbles over in John the Baptist's heart; even in the womb he cannot but jump for sheer exhilaration and wonderment.

Elizabeth calls Mary "she who has believed that the Lord [God] would fulfil his promises to her" (v 45). This is what we thought about yesterday. God speaks, and Mary believes and obeys. And great blessing follows.

This certainly says something to us about the real and human life of precious babies in the womb. They don't become human at birth. They can—in ways we can only discern in shadowy form—think and feel, hope and fear, delight and grieve. And who dares to put a start date on the genesis of that real humanness, unless it be the moment of conception? This vivid "baby in the womb" drama certainly makes us wonder at the mystery of every other baby growing so secretly in the mother's womb. Here is a life to be nurtured and treasured and guarded and prayed for. It's worth asking ourselves if there are ways in which we too can help others to nurture and treasure an unborn life, in a world that sometimes holds them cheap.

But there is also something unique about this. John the Baptist will be the last prophet, the final spokesman, of the old-covenant era. In his preaching he will be the summing-up witness for the Old Testament. And everything about his preaching will point to one man, and one man alone. We know this from what the Gospels teach us of his public ministry. But here, even before he is born, his whole tiny being leaps for joy in the presence of the only-just-conceived Jesus. In this lovely moment, we learn that the whole of the Old Testament, as it were, jumps for joy in the presence of the One to whom it has pointed, for whom it has longed for all these centuries of waiting. All the longings of the Old Testament feed that joyful jump of John the Baptist!

May our hearts never be slow to leap for joy at the wonder and truth of Jesus. Pray that you would know the thrill and delight of this King more and more this Christmas, and beyond.

∽SING

> *Joy to the world, the Lord has come!*
> *Let earth receive her King,*
> *Let every heart prepare him room,*
> *And heaven and nature sing,*
> *And heaven and nature sing,*
> *And heaven, and heaven, and nature sing!*
>
> *Joy to the earth! The Saviour reigns:*
> *Let men their songs employ;*
> *While fields and floods, rocks, hills, and plains*
> *Repeat the sounding joy,*
> *Repeat the sounding joy,*
> *Repeat, repeat the sounding joy.*
> *(Isaac Watts, 1674-1748)*

˙PRAY

Almighty God, our heavenly Father, who by your Spirit caused the unborn John the Baptist to leap for joy in the presence of your incarnate Son, and then to spend his life in bearing testimony to that wonderful Son, grant to us a measure of the same Spirit-given jubilation as we too rejoice in Jesus, and the majesty and rescue that he brings. We ask it in Jesus' name, Amen.

JOURNAL

_____

_____

_____

_____

_____

_____

_____

_____

_____

_____

_____

_____

_____

_____

_____

_____

_____

_____

_____

_____

LUKE 1 v 46-55

⁴⁶ And Mary said:

"My soul glorifies the Lord
⁴⁷ and my spirit rejoices in God my Saviour,
⁴⁸ for he has been mindful of the humble state
of his servant.
From now on all generations will call me
blessed,
⁴⁹ for the Mighty One has done great things
for me—holy is his name.
⁵⁰ His mercy extends to those who fear him,
from generation to generation.
⁵¹ He has performed mighty deeds with his arm;
he has scattered those who are proud in their
inmost thoughts.
⁵² He has brought down rulers from their
thrones
but has lifted up the humble.
⁵³ He has filled the hungry with good things
but has sent the rich away empty.
⁵⁴ He has helped his servant Israel,
remembering to be merciful
⁵⁵ to Abraham and his descendants for ever,
just as he promised our ancestors."

10 GOOD THINGS FOR THE HUMBLE

When pregnant women meet, they will naturally speak about their expected babies. Nowadays they might chat about maternity leave and birthing plans and car seats and baby clothes. If they sing a song (which is, perhaps, a little unusual in our cultures), it is more likely that they will practice a lullaby than sing a psalm. We can perhaps imagine Mary singing "Somewhere over the rainbow" to Elizabeth's "bump", humming of a faraway land of blue skies, melting troubles and dreams come true.

But Mary, by the Holy Spirit, sings a much better song! Hers is not comforting make-believe but rock-solid gospel truth and wonder. (While the text doesn't actually say that this is a "song", the words are in the kind of poetry that might well have been sung.) It echoes the song of Hannah, the mother of Samuel (1 Samuel 2 v 1-10) and parts of Psalm 113. Mary's song became one of the best known in Christian history, often known by its first word in Latin: the "Magnificat". Her words are not so well-known today, but we would do well to sing them again.

The central theme is this: in the gospel of Mary's son God brings some down and raises others up.

Mary sings with astonishment, first, of how God has blessed her in her "humble state" (v 46-49). *I am a nobody,* she sings; *I deserve nothing; and yet God has raised me up and blessed me with this son; for the rest of human history people will remember how God has blessed me.* But then she goes on (v 50-53): *God will do for every man and woman who fears him what he has done for me.*

Always, in the gospel of Mary's son, God lifts up the humble—people with nothing to contribute, people who look unimpressive, people who are morally messed-up, people who are hungry (who, as Mary's son will later say, "hunger and thirst for righteousness", Matthew 5 v 6). *These* are the people God will fill with good things. If that is how you feel this Christmas, take heart: God promises to fill you with good things.

If you read this as someone who belongs to Mary's son, remember that, like her, you were an undeserving nobody. How quickly we forget that our talents, our exams, our successes in sport or work or family count for nothing. Yet God has reached down to us, as he did to the lowly Mary, and blessed us, in Mary's son, with every spiritual blessing. The Spirit helps Mary to grasp that she is experiencing the blessings of her son: blessings that will overflow to every man, woman, and child who belongs to Jesus.

But there's another side to Mary's song. There's a bringing down. Those who, deep in their inmost thoughts, are proud will be scattered—just as the proud builders of the Tower of Babel were scattered (Genesis 11 v 1-9). We may be proud in thinking too much of our achievements, which is pride fed by success; or we may, paradoxically, be proud in thinking too little of ourselves and wallowing in our failures, which is just pride disappointed. Often we'll swing between both of these. But however pride shows itself in us, we need to watch out. For Mary's son will scatter us. Whether we're proud people who love to sit on thrones, or rich people who care nothing for the poor, the gospel of Mary's son warns us to repent.

And so, as we sing this song with Mary, we rejoice at God's kindness to her, as it overflows through her wonderful son, to us; and we take warning to flee from pride.

ᶜSING

Of the Father's love begotten
Ere the worlds began to be,
He is Alpha and Omega;
He the source, the ending he,
Of the things that are, that have been,
And that future years shall see
Evermore and evermore!

O that birth forever blessed,
When a virgin, full of grace,
By the Holy Ghost conceiving,
Bore the Saviour of our race;
And the Babe, the world's Redeemer,
First revealed his sacred face,
Evermore and evermore!

O ye heights of heaven adore him,
Angel hosts, his praises sing,
Pow'rs, dominions, bow before him,
And extol our God and King;
Let no tongue on earth be silent,
Ev'ry voice in concert ring
Evermore and evermore!

(Aurelius Clemens Prudentius, 348-410
Translated by H.W. Baker, 1821-1877)

PRAY

God our Father, I reflect today that I can be proud of nothing; that all my achievements, my morality, my respectability, my reputation for being a good person count for nothing. I turn today from pride in my deepest heart, from thinking I am somebody, or that you owe me something because of my goodness. And I thank and praise you, as Mary did, that you have reached down to me in my helpless state, and by the wonder and mercy of Mary's son, the Lord Jesus, you have raised me up, forgiven my sins, and filled me with so many good things, in this life and for eternity. In Jesus' name, Amen.

JOURNAL

_____

_____

_____

_____

_____

_____

_____

_____

_____

_____

_____

_____

_____

_____

_____

_____

_____

_____

_____

_____

_____

LUKE 1 v 67-75

[After the birth of John the Baptist, his parents name him "John". Then his father is given back his voice, to sing a wonderful song—traditionally called the "Benedictus" (after its first word in Latin). We are going to spend three days meditating on some of its themes.]

⁶⁷ [John's] father Zechariah was filled with the Holy Spirit and prophesied:

⁶⁸ "Praise be to the Lord, the God of Israel,
   because he has come to his people and
   redeemed them.
⁶⁹ He has raised up a horn of salvation for us
   in the house of his servant David
⁷⁰ (as he said through his holy prophets of
   long ago),
⁷¹ salvation from our enemies
   and from the hand of all who hate us—
⁷² to show mercy to our ancestors
   and to remember his holy covenant,
⁷³ the oath he swore to our father Abraham:
⁷⁴ to rescue us from the hand of our enemies,
   and to enable us to serve him without fear
⁷⁵ in holiness and righteousness before him all
   our days."

11 RESCUE FROM ENEMIES

hristmas is about rescue from bitter enemies. "No!" say the Christmas movies, the Christmas decorations, the Christmas songs playing in the shopping malls. No, Christmas is all about goodwill and peace and everybody being nice to one another. Christmas is about friendship, neighbourliness, family cheer and kissing under the mistletoe. It has nothing to do with enmity. Don't spoil Christmas by talking about hatred.

Ah, but we must. Christmas is about the people of God being rescued from those who hate them. Zechariah's boy will announce a great rescue. Zechariah, filled with the Holy Spirit, sings of God's people being "redeemed" (v 68), a word which harks back to when the Israelites were brought out of slavery in the Egypt of the Pharaohs. He sings of "a horn of salvation"—which means a strong rescuer—"in the house of [God's] servant David": that is, a King in David's line (v 69). This rescuer will be a strong King to set God's people free. Zechariah celebrates the arrival of "salvation from our enemies and from the hand of all who hate us" and "rescue ... from the hand of our enemies" (v 71, 74). He delights in the hope that at last God's people will be free "to serve him without fear" (v 74), just as the Hebrew slaves in Egypt were set free to worship the Lord their God at Mount Sinai after the exodus.

But what does this mean? Many reading this will not feel that they are surrounded by people who hate them (although some will). We may want to skim over this part of Zechariah's song and get on to the bits that connect with our experience. Yet to do so would be foolish, for every Christian has a great enemy, who is a murderer and a liar and the father of lies (John 8 v 44). He tempted Adam and Eve so that they walked head first into the shadow of death. Satan loves to steal and kill and destroy. He spoils lives with sin, with sickness, with fighting, with bitterness, and ultimately with death. The devil is a real and terrible enemy.

But there is more. What the Bible sometimes calls "the world"—men and women living in God's world without submitting to God, loving God or caring about God— has in its heart a deep hostility to all who belong to God and to God's Son, the King in David's line. Right back near the beginning of Genesis, Cain hated his brother Abel, because Abel was a man of faith who trusted God (Genesis 4; 1 John 3 v 12). And Cain set the tone for a long and dark tradition of hostility towards those who truly belong to God. Many of our brothers and sisters around the world know what it is to face bitter persecution and hatred for belonging to Jesus Christ. Some of us live in lands where that hostility lies below the surface; we must not be surprised when it comes out into the open. And we must remember that all of us were by nature among those enemies before Jesus laid his hand on us and made us God's friends.

Yet there is an even closer enemy than the devil and the world. Right inside ourselves, like a spy or terrorist who infiltrates our very heart, what the Bible calls our "flesh" fights against our souls and spiritual lives. We face bitter hostility from the world, the flesh and the devil. And Jesus came to rescue us! "The reason the Son of God appeared was to destroy the devil's work" (1 John 3 v 8). The more deeply we are aware of these enemies, the more we will join Zechariah in glad songs of praise. Jesus came at the first Christmas so that by his obedient life and his sin-bearing death, he might rescue us from all our enemies.

Take time out to think: In what ways do you feel the oppression of the world, the flesh and the devil today? How does it most hurt? In what ways can you feel dark hostility? Remember: Christmas is about enemies! But thank God: Jesus has come. And hold on: he is coming soon (Revelation 22 v 12).

ᶜSING

O come, O come, Emmanuel,
And ransom captive Israel,
That mourns in lonely exile here,
Until the Son of God appear.
Rejoice! Rejoice! Emmanuel
Shall come to thee, O Israel.

O come, thou Rod of Jesse, free
Thine own from Satan's tyranny;
From depths of hell thy people save,
And give them victory o'er the grave.
Rejoice! Rejoice! Emmanuel
Shall come to thee, O Israel.

O come, thou Dayspring, from on high,
And cheer us by thy drawing nigh;
Disperse the gloomy clouds of night,
And death's dark shadows put to flight.
Rejoice! Rejoice! Emmanuel
Shall come to thee, O Israel.

O come, thou Key of David, come
And open wide our heav'nly home;
Make safe the way that leads on high,
And close the path to misery.
Rejoice! Rejoice! Emmanuel
Shall come to thee, O Israel.

(Unknown)

PRAY

Our Father, as we long for that day when we will finally be set free from all our enemies, we pray for many of those enemies of the gospel to become friends of God, as Saul of Tarsus was so wonderfully converted; and we cry, with the church of every age, "Come, Lord Jesus!" And we rejoice as we hear his answering call: "I am coming soon!" Amen.

JOURNAL

_____

_____

_____

_____

_____

_____

_____

_____

_____

_____

_____

_____

⁶⁷ [John's] father Zechariah was filled with the Holy Spirit and prophesied:

⁶⁸ "Praise be to the Lord, the God of Israel,
   because he has come to his people and
   redeemed them.
⁶⁹ He has raised up a horn of salvation for us
   in the house of his servant David
⁷⁰ (as he said through his holy prophets of
   long ago),
⁷¹ salvation from our enemies
   and from the hand of all who hate us—
⁷² to show mercy to our ancestors
   and to remember his holy covenant,
⁷³ the oath he swore to our father Abraham:
⁷⁴ to rescue us from the hand of our enemies,
   and to enable us to serve him without fear
⁷⁵ in holiness and righteousness before him all
   our days."

AN ANCIENT PROMISE
REMEMBERED

Christmas is God keeping a promise. Christmas had to happen, because God had promised that it would. So often, it is not like that with us. "Last Christmas, I gave you my heart," goes the jilted lover's song. But you know what happens the very next day…

Plenty of tears will be shed this Christmas for broken promises: marriage vows cast away, business commitments reneged on, pledges of care for elderly parents or young children lying torn up on the floor like discarded wrapping paper. Maybe your life is littered with the debris of a broken promise, and it hurts so much. Perhaps you feel the dreadful guilt of a promise you yourself have broken, knowing that others are hurting. But—most wonderfully—God is utterly faithful and keeps his promises without fail. Christmas—properly understood—brings comfort to the casualties of broken promises.

Yesterday, I missed out an important part of Zechariah's song. It's in verses 72-73. Zechariah sings that, with the coming of the baby whom his son will announce, God will "show mercy" to the ancestors of the people of God, and will "remember his holy covenant, the oath he swore" to their forefather, the patriarch Abraham.

More than a thousand years before the first Christmas, God solemnly swore an oath to Abraham. We read about it first in Genesis 12, and then again and again through the book of Genesis and beyond. It was a promise, a vow, a covenant—which means a solemn agreement into which God chose to enter. He promised Abraham that his "offspring" or "seed"—someone descended from him—would inherit the world, would bring blessing to the world, would rule the world.

All down the years of Old Testament history that promise resonated. In all the ups and downs (mostly downs) of the people of God, they remembered that God had made this promise to Abraham. And they believed—or at least some of them believed—that what God had promised God would perform. One day God would put the whole world to rights through one of Abraham's descendants. But who would it be?

To "remember" in the Bible means more than just calling something to mind; it means remembering and acting on what is remembered. When God "remembers" his promise, it doesn't mean he has previously forgotten it; it means he takes some action to bring about what he has promised.

When God redeemed the people from slavery under the Pharaohs, he was remembering his promise to Abraham. When he brought them into the promised land, he was keeping the vow he had made to Abraham. When he gave them David the king, he was acting on his solemn oath. And yet all these little mercies and rescues pointed forward to one great final keeping of the covenant. On that day the "seed" of Abraham—one wonderful man, God incarnate—came to earth and took upon himself a fully human nature in order to live for, love and die for sinners, and be raised from the dead. This astonishing, unique man, whose birth we remember at Christmas, is the seed of Abraham. In him all the promises of God say their resounding "Yes!" (2 Corinthians 1 v 20) Jesus Christ is God keeping his covenant to Abraham.

And so, amid the misery of broken promises and shattered dreams, when we despair of our own unfaithfulness to our promises, take heart that at Christmas God has kept his covenant promise to Abraham.

ᴄSING

See, amid the winter's snow,
Born for us on earth below,
See, the tender Lamb appears,
Promised from eternal years.

Hail, thou ever blessed morn!
Hail redemption's happy dawn!
Sing through all Jerusalem,
Christ is born in Bethlehem.

Sacred Infant, all divine,
What a tender love was thine,
Thus to come from highest bliss
Down to such a world as this!
(Edward Caswall, 1814-1878)

PRAY

God our Father, we praise and thank you that in a world where promises are broken, you have never broken one of yours. We thank you that in the birth, life, death and resurrection of Jesus Christ, you have said a resounding and eternal "Yes!" to every promise of your word. Thank you for the worldwide scope of your covenant with Abraham. Thank you for the promise of blessing to the world. Thank you that, belonging to Jesus, we inherit the blessings of that covenant. In Jesus' name, Amen.

JOURNAL

76 "And you, my child, will be called a prophet
of the Most High;
for you will go on before the Lord to
prepare the way for him,
77 to give his people the knowledge of
salvation
through the forgiveness of their sins,
78 because of the tender mercy of our God,
by which the rising sun will come to us
from heaven
79 to shine on those living in darkness
and in the shadow of death,
to guide our feet into the path of peace."

80 And the child grew and became strong in
spirit; and he lived in the wilderness until he
appeared publicly to Israel.

LIGHT IN
THE DARKNESS

What goes through your mind when you see homes decorated with Christmas lights? Do you smile at the cheery colours in the darkness? Or maybe you think that the display of flashing reindeer isn't quite your style! Yet even before the invention of the LED, Christmas was always been about light. It still is. But not the sort of light you store away in a cupboard and get out once a year. No, this is a better light by far.

When John the Baptist's father sings of "the rising sun" coming to us "from heaven to shine on those living in darkness" (v 78-79), he really has something to sing about. He is singing to his baby boy ("And you, my child...", v 76) about the message he will so courageously declare when he grows up. John will go ahead of the Lord Jesus, God himself in human flesh, with a message of light in darkness.

And what darkness it is. These lines in Zechariah's song hint at the intimate connection between sin and death.

When Zechariah sings about the darkness of "the shadow of death", we all understand that (v 79). When someone we dearly love dies, Christmas becomes such a poignant and painful time. The empty chair, the empty bed, the empty silence—it all cries "Woe!" in the darkness. We feel the presence of death in every sickness too; even something trivial like a bruise or a cold is the outer edge of the shadow of death. Each year as we get older, we feel the tentacles of the encroaching darkness. Sadness of mind, the troubled heart, the painful body all shout to us, "You are going to die!" And it hurts. Even our joyful days, the days full of light, are never free of some shadow of worry or doubt or fear.

But what can shine a true light upon us who dwell in the shadow of death? The comfort of fantasy may dull the pain for an evening, but it can give no lasting light. To feel the true light we need, first, to grasp the true problem.

And the heart of our pain is not death but sin. It is our sin that brought death into existence (Romans 5 v 12-21). When Adam and Eve set their hearts against the God of life, and were marched out of paradise, death entered the world. You and I share in their sin. Our default heart-setting is much more serious than we like to think. We die because we are sinners. We cannot say that individual sufferings are the consequence of particular sins—at least, not all the time; sometimes they may be. But we can say that the shadow of death falls on us because it is the completely fair and just judgment of God upon a world of wilful sinners.

Once we grasp that—and only when we grasp that—there can be hope. For the message John the Baptist brought, the message of Jesus Christ, is "the forgiveness of ... sins" through "the tender mercy of our God" (v 77-78). It was John the Baptist's costly privilege to walk ahead of the Saviour and to announce loudly and clearly that in this Saviour our sins can be forgiven. There is no better news. For men and women with awakened consciences, burdened by the guilt of hearts centred on ourselves, haunted by memories—perhaps especially at Christmas—of things said and done of which we are ashamed, there can be nothing more wonderful to hear than this: our sins can be forgiven. And they can. It is true. This is not fantasy. Because Jesus Christ came in human flesh, and lived, and grew, and loved God, and died to pay the penalty for sinners, our sins can really be forgiven.

And that means that while the shadow of death still falls on our bodies in this life, if we belong to Christ, our spirits are raised with him (Ephesians 2 v 6). When you feel the shadow of death cast its dark gloom over your life, know for sure that the light has dawned. And rejoice that one day we too will be raised in new bodies in the new creation, and death will be no more.

SING

Hark! A thrilling voice is sounding;
"Christ is nigh," it seems to say;
"Cast away the works of darkness,
O ye children of the day!"

Lo, the Lamb, so long expected,
Comes with pardon down from heaven;
Let us haste, with tears of sorrow,
One and all, to be forgiven;

That when next he comes with glory,
And the world is wrapped in fear,
With his mercy he may shield us,
And with words of love draw near.
　　　(Translated by Edward Caswall, 1814-1878)

PRAY

God our Father, when we feel the cold darkness of the shadow of death, draw our minds and hearts from the sadness to our sin, that we may come to Jesus, your only Son, to be forgiven; and through him, who is the Light of the world, may we rejoice in sins forgiven and the sure and certain hope of death defeated. We ask it for Jesus' sake, Amen.

JOURNAL

_____

_____

_____

_____

_____

_____

_____

_____

_____

_____

_____

_____

_____

_____

_____

_____

_____

_____

LUKE 2 v 1-7

[1] In those days Caesar Augustus issued a decree that a census should be taken of the entire Roman world. [2] (This was the first census that took place while Quirinius was governor of Syria.) [3] And everyone went to their own town to register. [4] So Joseph also went up from the town of Nazareth in Galilee to Judea, to Bethlehem the town of David, because he belonged to the house and line of David. [5] He went there to register with Mary, who was pledged to be married to him and was expecting a child. [6] While they were there, the time came for the baby to be born, [7] and she gave birth to her firstborn, a son. She wrapped him in cloths and placed him in a manger, because there was no guest room available for them.

THE SHADOW OF
THE CROSS

Few things have caught our collective imagination more vividly than these traditional words: "There was no room for them in the inn" (v 7, KJV). Crib scenes all over the world show the infant Jesus lying in a manger under the rough roof of a stable, with farm animals in attendance. And in the background we might imagine a choir of small children singing:

> *Away in a manger, no crib for a bed,*
> *The little Lord Jesus laid down his sweet head.*
> *The stars in the night sky looked down where he*
> *lay [almost in the open air?]—*
> *The little Lord Jesus asleep on the hay.*
> *The cattle are lowing...*

But, while it all seems very sweet, there's a problem: with the facts, with the reason behind them, and with why they matter.

So far as the facts are concerned—and one feels like a party-pooper in saying this—the word traditionally translated "inn" more likely means something like "guest room" (as the NIV now translates it). And, while the "manger" really does mean an animal's feeding trough, there is no evidence that animals were present at Jesus' birth. They may have been or they may not. But there is something so simple about Luke's description: Mary's time came, she gave birth (and what pain and courage are represented in those three words), and she wrapped her son in swaddling cloths and placed him in an animal's feeding trough. Although our crib scenes add imaginative details, the picture of a scene of simplicity and poverty is right.

But what does it mean to say that "there was no guest room available for them"? After all, in most half-decent societies, all sorts of people would make space for a pregnant woman about to give birth. So why didn't these people? Why, in Bethlehem, did no one take pity on Mary so that she might give birth with some privacy and safety? We don't know. Maybe the people in Bethlehem were a deeply and universally uncaring and heartless crowd. That's possible. Or, perhaps more likely, it might be that some word of the unusual circumstances of the pregnancy had gone around—the whisper that this young pregnant woman had got into that condition before marriage to her respectable fiancé Joseph. Maybe this is why Mary was, rather literally, frozen out of Bethlehem society. Certainly, three decades or so later, in Jesus' adult life, people still made pointed comments hinting at his scandalous origins: "We are not illegitimate children," they protested to Jesus (John 8 v 41), with perhaps a sneer and the unspoken words, *Not like you*. The virgin conception of Jesus is a wonderful thing; but for Mary just then, and for Mary and Jesus thereafter, it was more likely to be understood as a scandal.

Whatever the reason—and we cannot know for sure—we should meditate on the significance of what happened. Right at the very beginning of Jesus' life on earth, from the moment of his birth, "the Son of Man [had] nowhere to lay his head"—nowhere decent and comfortable, at least (Luke 9 v 58). From his first breath—with only an animal's feeding trough for a bed—to his last breath—naked and disgraced, in agony on a Roman cross—the Son of God knew what it was to become very, very poor. And why? So that we through his poverty might become rich (2 Corinthians 8 v 9).

The Lord Jesus was poor for us, marginalised for us, excluded for us, frozen out of polite society for us. And by his obedient, costly life and his obedient, sin-bearing death, we are made unimaginably rich.

And yet he calls us to take up our cross daily (Luke 9 v 23). We ought not—we must not—contrive a life that is more comfortable than our Saviour's, even at Christmas time. So what would it look like for you to take up your cross today? Perhaps you will invite a neighbour to a Christmas service, knowing you risk their painful rejection; or you'll avoid excess at a Christmas party even though others laugh at you; or you will speak of Jesus with unbelieving family members, even though you know it will be awkward. When you experience just a little painful exclusion, take heart as you remember that this was the experience of Jesus from the first seconds of his life on earth.

♫SING

> *Thou who wast rich beyond all splendour,*
> *All for love's sake becamest poor;*
> *Thrones for a manger didst surrender,*
> *Sapphire-paved courts for stable floor.*
> *Thou who wast rich beyond all splendour,*
> *All for love's sake becamest poor.*
>
> *Thou who art God beyond all praising,*
> *All for love's sake becamest man;*
> *Stooping so low, but sinners raising*
> *Heavenwards by thine eternal plan.*
> *Thou who art God beyond all praising,*
> *All for love's sake becamest man.*
>
> (Frank Houghton, 1894-1972)

PRAY

God our Father, whose Son, our Lord Jesus Christ, began his life on earth in a wooden feeding trough and ended it on a Roman cross, we thank you for his immeasurable love towards us in becoming so poor, that we might be made so rich; we praise you for the forgiveness of our sins, for our sure and certain hope of glory, for the assurance of your unfailing love towards us day by day in Jesus. And we ask that you will give us grace not to be surprised when we are marginalised for his sake, and to have courageous faith to walk in his footsteps. For Jesus' sake, Amen.

JOURNAL

LUKE 2 v 8-11

[8] And there were shepherds living out in the fields near by, keeping watch over their flocks at night. [9] An angel of the Lord appeared to them, and the glory of the Lord shone around them, and they were terrified. [10] But the angel said to them, "Do not be afraid. I bring you good news that will cause great joy for all the people. [11] Today in the town of David a Saviour has been born to you; he is the Messiah, the Lord. [12] This will be a sign to you: you will find a baby wrapped in cloths and lying in a manger."

15
VICTORY IN WEAKNESS

The shepherds are part and parcel of our traditional nativity scene. Countless children have had tea towels wrapped around their heads to make up the numbers of "shepherds". Once the teacher has cast Mary and Joseph, and found a doll to be "Jesus", well, there are always the shepherds to mop up the children who don't yet have a part. In truth they are more like sheep than shepherds; they need to be herded around! But never mind; it is all part of the Christmas excitement.

And so the motley crew of shepherds gathers round the manger, gazing down at the cute, tiny, adorable newborn "baby" within. Perhaps this is why Christmas feels less threatening to us than Good Friday and Easter; for the one at the centre of the story is so sweet. I can look down on him, coo over him, caress him.

Or can I?

If we properly listen to the angels, then we may be in for a surprise. First we hear from one angel (today), and then a whole company of angels (tomorrow). This first angel's message to the shepherds seems to be contradicted by the "sign" that is supposed to show them it's true.

Here's the message: "I bring you good news" (v 10)—literally, "I am gospelling you". In the ancient world a "gospel" was the announcement of a new government. When a new king took over a country, messengers went through the land proclaiming the "gospel" of this new ruler. So who's the ruler? He arrives in "the town of David" (Bethlehem); he's going to be "a Saviour"; he is "the Messiah" (or "Christ"), "the Lord" (v 11). So he's a king—*the* King in David's line, the great Ruler promised all down the Old Testament years. And, precisely because he will be a powerful Ruler, he will be the Saviour of all God's people.

Because he is strong, he can save; he can only be "Saviour" because he is Ruler. Only a powerful King is strong enough to rescue us from the oppressive powers that enslave. Moses needed the power of God to rescue God's people from the enslaving Pharaoh. This King will need all the power of God to save men and women from the devil and all the dark forces of evil in the universe. You and I cannot break free from the slavery of sin because "everyone who sins is a slave to sin" (John 8 v 34)—and we all sin. We need a strong Lord if we are to have a true Saviour.

If the shepherds had any sort of belief in the Old Testament Scriptures, they would have had at least a vague idea that one day God would send the Messiah, the King, the Saviour. But how can they know that at last that day has come? Answer: the angel gives them a sign.

What kind of "sign"? Presumably something impressive and strong—something to make these shepherds gasp with shock and awe.

Yet here is the "sign": "you will find a baby wrapped in cloths and lying in a manger" (Luke 2 v 12). It would be hard to find a more disappointing sign! Everything is wrong! It's a baby: an infant "wrapped in cloths", swaddling clothes, which means it must be a newborn baby. And—as every new parent knows—nothing is more helpless than a newborn. You have to do everything— but *everything*—for a baby. They can't walk, they can't talk, they can't crawl, they can't even lift up their heads! More than that, the sign is a baby lying in an animal's feeding trough. There's no expensive crib for this little boy; he is born of a poor mother, excluded from society, unimpressive in every way. Nothing, but nothing, about this sign suggests that he is the King, the Messiah, the Lord, the Saviour.

Ah, but it does. In the poignant music of his birth, we hear the sad melody of his death. And by that weak death he will defeat all the powers of evil, will be crowned as Messiah and Lord, will be the strong Saviour of all who will trust in him. This sign is precisely right. It is by his weakness that he is strong, by his vulnerability that he is the conqueror, by his sufferings that he will be the Saviour. Marvel with the shepherds at this conquering baby, this meek Messiah, this despised Lord.

As you marvel, consider also that you are called to walk in his footsteps. Strength, success and impressiveness we long for; yet weakness, discouragement and vulnerability is the way of the manger.

SING

*Hark! The herald-angels sing,
"Glory to the newborn king;
Peace on earth and mercy mild,
God and sinners reconciled."
Joyful, all ye nations rise,
Join the triumph of the skies;
With the angelic host proclaim,
"Christ is born in Bethlehem."
Hark! The herald-angels sing,
"Glory to the new-born king"*

*Christ, by highest heaven adored,
Christ, the everlasting Lord;
Late in time behold him come,
Offspring of a Virgin's womb.
Veiled in flesh the Godhead see,
Hail the incarnate Deity,
Pleased as man with man to dwell,
Jesus, our Emmanuel.
Hark! The herald-angels sing,
"Glory to the new-born king"*

(Charles Wesley, 1707-1788)

PRAY

God our Father, whose Son, the Lord Jesus, came to this earth in great weakness and died in great agony, bearing our sins, we thank you for his amazing love and wonderful condescension. Fill our hearts, we pray, as you filled the hearts of the shepherds, with wonder, love and praise. For Jesus' sake, Amen.

JOURNAL

LUKE 2 v 13-18

¹³ Suddenly a great company of the heavenly host appeared with the angel, praising God and saying,

¹⁴ "Glory to God in the highest heaven, and on earth peace to those on whom his favour rests."

¹⁵ When the angels had left them and gone into heaven, the shepherds said to one another, "Let's go to Bethlehem and see this thing that has happened, which the Lord has told us about."

¹⁶ So they hurried off and found Mary and Joseph, and the baby, who was lying in the manger. ¹⁷ When they had seen him, they spread the word concerning what had been told them about this child, ¹⁸ and all who heard it were amazed at what the shepherds said to them.

16 GLORY AND PEACE

If a Christmas card competition were to count which Bible verses are used on the most cards, I wonder if these words would top the poll: "Glory to God in the highest heaven, and on earth peace to those on whom his favour rests" (v 14). But if these words are among the best known, I wonder also if they are among those least considered. When I see them on a card, I do not usually give them a second thought. They register with me no more than berries on a holly branch or tinsel on a tree.

But I want to invite you to pause and think with me about these words. For they are not just the stocking-fillers of angelic choirs—what angels sing when they can't think of any other lyrics to use. They are the thoughtful, meaningful response of the great company of angels to the astonishing message of the one angel to which we listened yesterday. One angel announces the King, the Messiah, the Saviour, the newborn baby. And the company respond with this triumphant declaration of glory and peace.

They tell us that with the birth of this baby boy, something happens in two places.

First, in "the highest heaven". The highest heaven is not a place in this space-time universe. You can't find it with a spacecraft, no matter how many light years you may travel. No, the highest heaven is a vivid way of speaking about "God's place", where God dwells in unapproachable light: a "place" above and beyond this whole created universe. In this "place" the triune God dwells. Glory is the outward shining of God's inward being; it is when his invisible weighty majesty becomes somehow visible and tangible to his creatures.

So when the angels declare, "Glory to God in the highest heaven", they proclaim that, with the birth of this boy—who is the eternal Son of God—the invisible God has made himself visible. And even in the highest "place" glory shines in a way in which glory did not shine before. That is an astonishing thought, for we are not talking about earth; we are speaking about the heavenly places. In that wonderful place—where God's glory shines through all eternity—in some unimaginable way glory shines with greater unparalleled splendour when Jesus is born.

And, second, something happens "on earth": there is peace. Peace is a great shorthand word. It means, first, peace between humans and the God from whom we are by nature alienated. This boy, this King and Saviour, will be the Mediator who brings us back to God by his death, so that we enjoy peace with God (Romans 5 v 1). And, because our alienation from God is the root of all our troubles, that peace with God brings in its train peace between people. All over the world, men and women will be brought into peace with God and then into peace with one another. Have you seen this at first hand in your church this year? And all this by the birth of this newborn baby boy.

But there is one more thing to notice. Peace comes "to those on whom his favour rests". That is, God will choose who will come into his peace, and when, and how. God will decide. If you belong to Jesus the Saviour, you have that joyful privilege because the favour of God has rested upon you. You didn't deserve it; you didn't earn it; you simply received it. It is all God's sovereign kindness.

So today let us join the angelic chorus in singing glory to God, whose majesty shines out in Jesus; let us hear with joy the angels as they proclaim peace—peace with God and peace with unlikely people all over the world. And in all this we humbly admit that we deserve none of it; God's favour has rested upon us simply because God, in his great kindness, chose that it should.

SING

"To you, in David's town, this day
Is born, of David's line,
A Saviour, who is Christ the Lord,
And this shall be the sign" ...

Thus spake the seraph; and forthwith
Appeared a shining throng
Of angels, praising God, who thus
Addressed their joyful song:

"All glory be to God on high,
And on the earth be peace;
Goodwill henceforth from heaven to men
Begin and never cease."

Nahum Tate (1652-1715)
and Edith Sanford Tillotson (1876-1968)

PRAY

Gracious and triune God—Father, Son and Holy Spirit—we praise you that your glory shone out in highest heaven when Jesus the Son was born. We thank you for the most wonderful gift of peace with God and peace between people. We humbly bow before your kindness and acknowledge that all these blessings are your undeserved kindness to us in Jesus. We praise you in Jesus' name, Amen.

JOURNAL

_____

_____

_____

_____

_____

_____

_____

_____

_____

_____

_____

_____

_____

_____

_____

_____

_____

_____

_____

_____

_____

LUKE 2 v 18-20

[18] ... and all who heard it were amazed at what the shepherds said to them. [19] But Mary treasured up all these things and pondered them in her heart. [20] The shepherds returned, glorifying and praising God for all the things they had heard and seen, which were just as they had been told.

TREASURING AND PONDERING

Mary was one of the most beautiful young women the world has ever seen. We have, of course, no idea what she looked like. But I am not thinking about the outward beauty that we humans so over-value. Mary may or may not have been pretty in that way; we simply don't know. Instead I am thinking about the inner beauty that God values. It's what Peter calls the beauty "of your inner self, the unfading beauty of a gentle and quiet spirit, which is of great worth in God's sight" (1 Peter 3 v 4). God gave Mary that kind of beauty in spades.

When the shepherds told their story of the angels and then the baby, people were "amazed" (Luke 2 v 18). Of course they were; it was an astonishing story. The shepherds went back to their fields, "glorifying and praising God for all the things they had heard and seen, which were just as they had been told" (v 20). That was a good reaction, a fitting response.

Yet in between those verses Luke gives us a little comment about Mary: "But Mary...". Notice the "but": here is a different reaction. "But Mary treasured up all these things and pondered them in her heart" (v 19). I want you to ponder with me today about pondering, to meditate on meditating! There is something deep and beautiful about what Mary does.

The story of the shepherds caused what would be their equivalent of a local media sensation. People were amazed. But then the news cycle continued; before long something else filled the headlines, and the time came when people said to one another, *Do you remember that thing that happened with the shepherds at Bethlehem?* And someone replied, *Oh, yes, I think I remember something, but I can't quite recall what it was.* For them, the angels might as well have been a firework display in the sky— here one moment but gone the next. I don't know what the shepherds themselves made of it a week later, or a month afterwards, or as the years rolled by. Did they constantly think about it? If they were alive thirty years later, did they connect Jesus of Nazareth with that extraordinary night? We simply don't know. Nor do we know what Joseph made of it all. The little we do know about him is all good—we are told he was a righteous man (Matthew 1 v 19)—but we don't know much.

But there is something special about Mary. Twice Luke tells us that Mary treasured the things of Jesus and turned them over and over in her heart. Twelve years later, after the strange incident where Jesus stays behind in the temple, Luke says, "But his mother treasured all these things in her heart" (Luke 2 v 51). Those two comments are, I suppose, just samples of the typical response of Mary. Again and again, she pondered. In one sense Mary enjoyed the most intimate earthly relationship with Jesus that is possible for human beings—that of a mother and a baby who has been knitted together in her womb, who is born from her body, whom she nurses at the breast. Is there any more intimate relationship in this world? No one knew Jesus better than Mary did. And yet, when the angel announces Jesus' conception, Mary knows there is something about this baby that she can never fully know. And now on the night of his birth, he is the son she will know and yet never completely know. When the shepherds tell of the angels, Mary treasures the things that concern Jesus in her heart.

We are not to venerate Mary or pray to Mary. She would not have wanted that, as it would dishonour the son she treasured. But we are to follow her example of beautiful, thoughtful, pondering faith. Somehow, in her simplicity and humility, she grasped what much more sophisticated people have often failed to understand: that Jesus is to be treasured and pondered. Jesus cannot be understood like a theorem; he cannot simply be weighed in the balances of evidence (although there is a place for that); there is something so deep and wonderful about the person of Jesus that a lifetime of pondering will not suffice. We can both know him deeply and marvel that we cannot comprehend him totally. There is something so precious about Jesus and all he brings to us that we can never treasure him enough. So, today, treasure and ponder the things of Jesus. And not just today—make pondering Jesus the habit of a lifetime.

ᶜSING

> *Immensity, cloister'd in thy dear womb,*
> *Now leaves his well-beloved imprisonment.*
> *There he hath made himself to his intent*
> *Weak enough, now into our world to come.*
> *But O! for thee, for him, hath th'inn no room?*
> *Yet lay him in a stall, and from th'orient,*
> *Stars, and wise men will travel to prevent*
> *The effects of Herod's jealous general doom.*
> *Seest thou, my soul, with thy faith's eye, how he*
> *Which fills all place, yet none holds him, doth lie?*
> *Was not his pity towards thee wondrous high,*
> *That would have need to be pitied by thee?*
> *Kiss him, and with him into Egypt go,*
> *With his kind mother, who partakes thy woe.*
>
> (John Donne, 1572-1631)

˙PRAY

Almighty and all-wise God, give us grace to ponder like Mary, and to treasure Jesus, your wonderful Son, as Mary did. Save us, we pray, from ever taking Jesus for granted, from thinking that we understand him. Teach us the precious habit of meditating on Jesus and of counting Jesus as uncountable worth. For his name's sake, Amen.

JOURNAL

_____

_____

_____

_____

_____

_____

_____

_____

_____

_____

_____

_____

_____

_____

_____

_____

_____

_____

_____

_____

LUKE 2 v 21

21 On the eighth day, when it was time to circumcise the child, he was named Jesus, the name the angel had given him before he was conceived.

18
JESUS!

"So what is your baby called?" When we hear some-one has given birth, I guess we have two ques-tions. Here's the first: "Is 'it' a boy or a girl?" And the moment we say "it", we feel uneasy; we know that from the moment of conception, the baby is a boy or a girl. Apart from being human, that is the most fundamental thing about him or her. But then we ask, "And what is the baby's name?" Because, somehow, until the baby has a name, things feel incomplete. Of course, if we're inter-ested, we'll ask, "What did she weigh?" If we're brave, we'll ask, "How was the labour?" And if we're foolish, we'll ask, "Does he have his mother's nose?" But the gender and the name are the most important questions.

I have never been to a "gender reveal party", but I am told they are all the rage (I read of one recently that was so exuberant that it started a bush fire!). At a suita-ble stage of the pregnancy and after some scans, friends gather around the mother-to-be and the announcement is made, perhaps with blue or pink fireworks or smoke: "It's a girl!" or "It's a boy!"

Many expectant parents choose a name for the baby before she or he is born. Much time is spent perusing lists of possible names, thinking about names in the family, looking at the most and least popular names this year, and so on. But one thing is clear: it is the parents who choose the name. Grandparents, uncles, aunts, cousins may have opinions, but, if they are wise, they keep them to themselves!

Sometimes we ask parents why they chose a particular name. Perhaps it belonged to a great-grandfather or maybe they just liked it. But imagine a conversation like this: *So why did you call him Jesus? Did you and Joseph like the name? Was it in the family?* And the answer: *We had to call him Jesus, whether we liked the name or not. God sent a messenger to tell us that must be his name.* A surprised pause. *Oh, so was that just in the last few days after he was born?* And the reply: *No, it was before he was even conceived.* I have never heard a conversation like that!

Something similar had happened to the parents of John the Baptist (Luke 1 v 13). But for Jesus it meant even more. It shows not only that every day of his life was written in God's book (Psalm 139 v 16); it placards before the world that what this name means—Saviour (Matthew 1 v 21)—is what this child will be.

Some names mean things; others don't mean much. But Jesus, like Joshua in the Old Testament, means Saviour. He came to rescue. That is why the eternal Son took our human nature upon himself.

Christmas is not about sweetness or feeling good in the middle of winter. It is about rescue. Christianity is a rescue religion. Jesus came to save lost people, desperately needy people. The angel gave him that name before he was conceived so there could be no doubt about that. In his great book *The City of God*, the fifth-century bishop Augustine catalogues at some length the miseries of living as sinners in a world under sin (he also goes to great lengths to speak of God's kindnesses!). Then he writes that there is no escape from this life "other than through the grace of Christ, our Saviour, God and Lord. The very name Jesus shows this, for it means Saviour; and what he saves us from most of all is a life after this one which is more miserable still: an eternal life which is more like death than life."

From before that great moment of conception in the womb of the virgin Mary, it was the determined purpose of God—Father, Son and Holy Spirit—that the Son should take human nature and be our Saviour. Every time you say the name "Jesus", you can remind yourself of that.

⁀SING

> *How sweet the name of Jesus sounds*
> *In a believer's ear!*
> *It soothes his sorrows, heals his wounds,*
> *And drives away his fear.*

It makes the wounded spirit whole
And calms the troubled breast;
'Tis manna to the hungry soul,
And to the weary, rest.

Dear Name! the Rock on which I build,
My Shield and Hiding Place,
My never-failing Treas'ry filled
With boundless stores of grace!

Jesus! my Shepherd, Husband, Friend,
My Prophet, Priest, and King;
My Lord, my Life, my Way, my End,
Accept the praise I bring.

Weak is the effort of my heart,
And cold my warmest thought;
But when I see thee as thou art,
I'll praise thee as I ought.

Till then I would thy love proclaim
With every fleeting breath,
And may the music of thy name
Refresh my soul in death.

(John Newton, 1725-1807)

PRAY

God our Father, we thank you for that infinite love which sent your Son, Jesus, to take human flesh to be our Saviour. We thank you for that matchless devotion in the heart of the Son, who freely came to be our Saviour. We praise you for the unfathomable power of love in the heart of the Holy Spirit, by whose agency the Son took human flesh to be our Saviour. Give us, we pray, a deep sense of how much we need saving and a correspondingly intense gratitude for Jesus our Saviour. We ask it in his name, Amen.

JOURNAL

LUKE 2 v 22-25

²² When the time came for the purification rites required by the Law of Moses, Joseph and Mary took him to Jerusalem to present him to the Lord ²³ (as it is written in the Law of the Lord, "Every firstborn male is to be consecrated to the Lord"), ²⁴ and to offer a sacrifice in keeping with what is said in the Law of the Lord: "a pair of doves or two young pigeons".

²⁵ Now there was a man in Jerusalem called Simeon, who was righteous and devout. He was waiting for the consolation of Israel, and the Holy Spirit was on him.

WAITING WITH HOPE 19

Waiting is hard. Today all over the world children will be itchy and scratchy as they find it hard to wait for Christmas Day. "But why can't I have my presents *now*? I want them *now*," they cry.

And waiting isn't only hard for children. I'm sure that you are waiting for something just now too. Take a moment to consider what that might be. It is so hard to wait, perhaps in vain, for a marriage partner, for a child, for the salvation of a loved one, for reconciliation in a relationship, for healing from a disease, for health and hope. Waiting, waiting, waiting. Day after day. Nothing to show for it. Just waiting. It can feel like an eternity; it can hurt like hell. And indeed hell is just what it is like. For hell is an eternity of waiting in vain. Waiting can be a foretaste of the terrors of hell, for hell is waiting and waiting without hope.

We'll spend the next five days in the company of two people who knew how to wait with hope. Had there been

Oscars back then, I would have nominated them for Best
Supporting Actor and Actress in the Bible story. First,
today and tomorrow, Simeon. Perhaps an older man. We
know only three things about Simeon. He was "righteous
and devout", a real believer in the promises of God; he
"was waiting for the consolation of Israel"; and "the Holy
Spirit was on him" (v 25). The Holy Spirit, who prepared
a body for the Son of God, also prepared a people to wait
for him. For the Holy Spirit is the *personal* Spirit, the
third Person of the Godhead, and he puts a hopeful waiting into the hearts of the people of God.

Think particularly about those words "waiting for the
consolation of Israel". All his life Simeon had known
the promises of God, and he waited for God to do what
he had promised to do. Day after day. Week after week.
Month after month. Year after year... he waited. He
watched. He prayed. He hoped. He trusted. He waited
for "consolation". There was so much sadness; there were
such depths of misery, so many tears, a plethora of pain.
Disappointment was everywhere. People hoped for life
and found death; they longed for strength and were given
sickness; in place of harmony and peace there was strife
and hatred. All around Simeon saw this. And he didn't
just see it; he felt the pain. He longed for consolation: for
God to console, to bring comfort to a world in pain.

And he longed for consolation for "Israel", the people
of God—men and women who trusted the promises of
God. Centuries earlier God had promised to Abraham a
"seed" or "offspring" through whom the world would be
blessed. Simeon longed for this. Many years had passed

since God promised to David an heir who would be King of all the world. Simeon believed that one day this King would come. He knew that this King in David's line, this seed of Abraham, would be the one who would deal with sin, who would defeat death, who would destroy the works of the devil. But he had not yet come. And so Simeon waited.

That King has come. Tomorrow we will watch Simeon in his joy. But we too wait. We wait for this great sin-bearing King to return in glory. We long for him to come back. We know that all our groaning, every tear, each sadness will finally be ended only when he comes. And so we wait. Waiting is hard. It was hard for Simeon. He must have heard a little voice in his ear tempting him to doubt: *Will God really do this? Are you sure? It doesn't look like it just now.*

Think again about what you are waiting for. And then learn from Simeon how to turn waiting from hell into hope—how to wait with hope. Trust that God has never broken a word yet, and he never will. And like Simeon, pin all your hopes on the word of God and the Christ, who fulfils every promise of God.

∽SING

> *Come, thou long expected Jesus,*
> *Born to set thy people free;*
> *From our fears and sins release us,*
> *Let us find our rest in thee.*
> *Israel's strength and consolation,*

Hope of all the earth thou art;
Dear desire of every nation,
Joy of every longing heart.

Born thy people to deliver,
Born a child and yet a King,
Born to reign in us for ever,
Now thy gracious kingdom bring.
By thine own eternal Spirit
Rule in all our hearts alone;
By thine all sufficient merit
Raise us to thy glorious throne.

(Charles Wesley, 1707-1788)

PRAY

Almighty God our Heavenly Father, who set your Holy Spirit upon Simeon so that he could learn to wait and pray and hope and trust your promises, set your Holy Spirit upon us also that we may long for Christ's return and learn to wait. Help us especially, we pray, when some yearning in this life is painfully deep, and waiting is hard, when we groan for consolation; give us the working of your Holy Spirit in a special measure, that we may be men and women who know how to wait with hope. For Jesus' sake, Amen.

JOURNAL

_____

_____

_____

_____

_____

_____

_____

_____

_____

_____

_____

_____

_____

_____

_____

_____

_____

_____

LUKE 2 v 26-32

²⁶ It had been revealed to [Simeon] by the Holy Spirit that he would not die before he had seen the Lord's Messiah. ²⁷ Moved by the Spirit, he went into the temple courts. When the parents brought in the child Jesus to do for him what the custom of the Law required, ²⁸ Simeon took him in his arms and praised God, saying:

²⁹ "Sovereign Lord, as you have promised,
   you may now dismiss your servant in peace.
³⁰ For my eyes have seen your salvation,
³¹ which you have prepared in the sight of all
   nations:
³² a light for revelation to the Gentiles,
   and the glory of your people Israel."

GOOD NEWS FOR THE WORLD

20

Waiting, waiting, waiting. Day after day Simeon waited. God the Holy Spirit had revealed to him that he would see the Messiah, the Christ, before he died. So he waited. And waited. And waited. And then one day the Holy Spirit moved him to go into the temple courts. A poor, young couple came in to make the law's offering for their firstborn son. The courts were probably thronged with people, rather like Grand Central Station on a busy weekday. But somehow Simeon knew to go to this young couple, who presumably looked no different from countless other poor people.

May I hold your baby? he asks, as people push past and the busyness of the day bustles around them. *You may.* And so, in a moment that sends a tingle down my spine, this old believer gently takes the little boy in his arms. He has waited so long. But now he knows his wait was not in vain. It is an extraordinary moment for any of us—the first time we hold a little baby in our arms, cradling the floppy head, holding him or her close and safe. Such a bundle of tiny limbs and measureless possibilities. "What will this baby become?" we ask as we look into their eyes. "What will the future hold for them?" And yet somehow Simeon knows. This little boy with poor parents who perhaps speak with a rough Galilean accent, this boy who looks so ordinary—*this child* is the Lord's Messiah. The hopes and fears of all the years are met in this little bundle of life.

And so Simeon sings, as he holds the infant Jesus in his arms. And what a wonderful song! It will be known for most of the history of the Christian church as the "Nunc Dimittis" (after the first words of the song in Latin). It is not so well known today, but it should be.

I can die now, Simeon begins. *You can dismiss your servant in peace. All my waiting is at an end.* Why? *Because I have seen, with my own eyes, the one who is your salvation, your great rescue for humankind. He is for all nations, for the Gentiles* (the rest of the world) *and for Israel too.* One old man, one tiny baby, one place, one day, and yet in this baby is the only hope of rescue for the whole world, for each and every man and woman who has ever lived or will ever live until history ends.

Simeon waited. He did not wait in vain, for he saw the Lord Jesus Christ and held him in his arms. We too wait. We look back, at Christmas, to the first coming of Christ as a tiny baby. We remember on Good Friday his death for sinners. We rejoice on Easter Sunday in his bodily resurrection. We celebrate on Ascension Day his glorious ascension to the Father's right hand. We delight at Pentecost in the outpouring of the Holy Spirit to dwell in our hearts as the down payment of eternal life. And we look forward at Advent to Jesus' return. And we wait. And we wait.

And just as Simeon did not wait in vain, we too will not wait in vain. People will mock; folk will doubt his return. But one day he will come back, not as a baby but in visible glory to judge the world and rescue his people. All our little waitings, as hard as they may be—for healing, for reconciliation, for mental health, for peace, for joy and life—are taken up in the one great waiting, the expectation that governs them all: the longing for Jesus' return. In the delight and wonder of Simeon as he held the baby Jesus, we see the foretaste of the wonder and amazement that we shall feel when the Lord Jesus Christ appears in glory. And we are assured that our wait is not in vain.

SING

O little town of Bethlehem,
How still we see thee lie;
Above thy deep and dreamless sleep
The silent stars go by,
Yet in thy dark streets shineth
The everlasting Light;
The hopes and fears of all the years
Are met in thee tonight.

For Christ is born of Mary,
And gathered all above,
While mortals sleep, the angels keep
Their watch of wondering love;
O morning stars together,
Proclaim the holy birth,
And praises sing to God the King,
And peace to men on earth

How silently, how silently
The wondrous gift is given!
So God imparts to human hearts
The blessings of his heaven.
No ear may hear his coming,
But in this world of sin,
Where meek souls will receive him still,
The dear Christ enters in.

(Phillips Brooks, 1835-1893)

PRAY

Dear God our heavenly Father, may your good Spirit place in our hearts today the joyful assurance that you gave to waiting Simeon, that we may know deeply, in the midst of a troubled world, that our waiting will not be in vain. Fix our eyes above, where Christ is, seated at your right hand, and from where Christ will come in glory to judge the world and save all who are waiting for him in hope. For Jesus' sake, Amen.

JOURNAL

_____

_____

_____

_____

_____

_____

_____

_____

_____

_____

_____

_____

_____

_____

_____

_____

_____

_____

_____

LUKE 2 v 33-35

[33] The child's father and mother marvelled at what was said about him. [34] Then Simeon blessed them and said to Mary, his mother: "This child is destined to cause the falling and rising of many in Israel, and to be a sign that will be spoken against, [35] so that the thoughts of many hearts will be revealed. And a sword will pierce your own soul too."

21
DESTINY COSTS

The story of Simeon ends on a very strange note. Just imagine: you have met a young mother; you have cradled her tiny baby in your arms; you have spoken eloquently about this little boy's future; indeed, you have declared that he will bring light to the whole world and glory to his people! And then you speak to the mother, and you say what Simeon now says. A shadow is cast over this happy scene, and Simeon will leave the stage with a sharp poignancy.

Pause to consider what Simeon says—four things, in essence. First, that "this child is destined to cause the falling and rising of many in Israel" (v 34). That may mean *to cause some to fall and others to rise*; but, partly because of the unusual order (falling before rising), it is more likely to mean *causing some to fall and then, after falling, to rise*. This child will bring people down, humble them, and only then raise them up; he will cause some to die and then be raised. But their rising up can only come after being brought low. So it was in his lifetime, and so it is today.

Second, Simeon says that Mary's son will "be a sign that will be spoken against" (v 34). And so it proved. He was indeed a sign: he made the Father known, pointing men and women to the Father. But right from the start of Jesus' public ministry, people spoke against him. Bitterly, dishonestly, maliciously, they spoke against him. They said he did what he did by the power of the devil. They despised him, maligned him and mocked him. He was indeed a sign that was spoken against.

Then Simeon says that, because this child will be a sign that is spoken against, "the thoughts of many hearts will be revealed" (v 35). There will be something about this boy that tears away the curtains of deception and self-deception from human hearts. He will do a work that reveals and changes the human heart. You and I have many strategies for disguising the deepest thoughts and intentions, desires and hopes, of our hearts. We disguise them even from ourselves. The human heart is deep and deceitful. But this boy will peel back the disguises, the hypocrisies, the pretences to reveal the human heart in its true nature. And he will change that heart.

But this work of bringing people down that he may raise them up, this ministry of being a sign pointing to the Father, this radical life-changing work in the human heart will come at a great cost. And so Simeon looks Mary in the eye and says to this hopeful young mother,

"A sword will pierce your own soul too" (v 35). What a terrible word to have to speak to a young woman at a time of her life that most obviously speaks of hope! *It's going to hurt you terribly. You will love this boy more deeply perhaps than you love any human being on earth. But in three decades time you will stand as a grief-stricken witness at a Roman crucifixion. And in that place of ugliness, agony, misery, shame and nakedness, you will watch your son die the most terrible death. You will see the sun go dark. You will feel the earth shake. And a sword will pierce your heart.*

And that's because the work that Mary's boy will do comes at an awesome cost. He can only be light by entering darkness; he can only save sinners by bearing wrath; he can only be glorious with the glory of God's self-giving love.

And so, right from the very earliest days of Jesus' life on earth, the shadow of the cross falls upon him and upon all who love him. For the sword that pierces Mary's heart will make its terrible sharpness felt in all who love Jesus, upon whom the shadow of his cross falls in daily dying to self. The Christian life is one of joy; but it is also one of pierced hearts. Don't be surprised when putting others first hurts; when obedience seems costly; when letting go of past grievances feels painful. But it is in our taking up of the cross, in filling up in our own persons what has to be filled up of the sufferings of Christ, that his light shines to the world (Colossians 1 v 24).

❂SING

All you that pass by,
To Jesus draw nigh;
To you is it nothing
That Jesus should die?
Your ransom and peace,
Your surety he is;
Come, see if there ever
Was sorrow like his.

(Charles Wesley, 1707-1788)

❂PRAY

Almighty God our heavenly Father, upon whose Son, the Lord Jesus, fell the shadow of the cross from the moment of his incarnation, we thank you for the wonderful love in your heart, which you share with the Son and the Holy Spirit, as we ponder the cost of our salvation. Give us, we pray, deeply grateful hearts and strengthen us to pay the cost of walking in the footsteps of such a Saviour. For Jesus' sake, Amen.

JOURNAL

_____

_____

_____

_____

_____

_____

_____

_____

_____

_____

_____

_____

_____

_____

_____

_____

_____

_____

_____

LUKE 2 v 36-37

[36] There was also a prophet, Anna, the daughter of Penuel, of the tribe of Asher. She was very old; she had lived with her husband seven years after her marriage, [37] and then was a widow until she was eighty-four. She never left the temple but worshipped night and day, fasting and praying.

22
SERIOUSLY HOPING

What is it that you are hoping for this Christmas? Precious family time? A triumphant Christmas dinner? The salvation of a loved one? Peace on earth? Or just a corner of peace and quiet?

If Simeon is Best Supporting Actor for the Bible story, then I vote for Anna as Best Supporting Actress. Today and tomorrow we will watch her. She has a small role but one pregnant with hope. She appears in these two verses alone in the Bible. But what a picture we are given of this remarkable old lady, and how lovely she is! She is "a prophet" (v 36); this means the Holy Spirit is at work through her so that she speaks the words that God wants spoken. That is remarkable enough, given the long silence of prophecy since the days of Malachi at the end of the Old Testament period—perhaps four centuries or so of silence. She is a genuine Israelite. We are given her father's name and that of her tribe; this is a way of telling us that she carries some weight and really belongs to the people of God. But she is not just a Jew outwardly and ethnically; she is a Jew spiritually, a believer in the promises of God (Romans 2 v 28-29).

And, Luke tells us, she is "very old". She certainly is! She married, presumably as a young woman, but sadly her husband died after just seven years of marriage. And now she is eighty-four (or possibly even older, if the eighty-four refers to her years of widowhood). Even today that counts as quite senior. In Anna's day that was a great old age. And a long widowhood. How sad! And yet there is a most remarkable hope infusing her sadness with the scent of great joy.

For this lovely believing widow "never left the temple but worshipped night and day, fasting and praying" (v 37). She comes to the place that was the focus of all the promises of God; for under the old covenant, the temple was just that. She bows down in her heart before the great God of Israel, the God of Abraham, the God of Isaac, the God of Jacob, who made those promises. Night and day she worships. She has devoted her long widowhood to prayer and adoration of the God of the covenant promises. And she fasts, as a natural expression of the seriousness of her commitment to give herself to prayer.

What is it she prays for? She prays for God to send his Messiah, his Christ. She prays for God to send the baby boy whom Simeon at this moment holds in his arms, and whom she will herself meet very soon.

Yet in her worshipping, fasting and praying, Anna demonstrates to us how to wait with hope and how to hope with seriousness. For Anna it is not a matter of a vague "Oh, I hope it will all be alright in the end". No, she grasps that God has chosen to bring about what he has promised through the prayers of his people. By his Spirit God causes a great desire to well up in the hearts of believers and pour itself out in passionate prayers.

Anna gives herself to prayer. She is serious about prayer. Her fasting is not to twist God's arm but an expression of how much her praying means to her; she will do anything to avoid being distracted, diverted, turned aside from prayer. She does not focus on her fasting; she fasts in order to devote herself to prayer. She knows that God has chosen not to fulfil his promises until and unless his people pray. And so she prays that God will do what he has promised to do. In the deep wisdom of God, this beautiful widow is drawn by the Spirit right into the purposes of God, so that the coming of the Messiah is, in part, the answer to her prayers.

No doubt you look towards Christmas with deep and unspoken hopes of all sorts and sizes. Are you submitting them to God in serious prayer, as Anna did? It is when we pray that God acts. But Anna's example refocuses our hopes too. You and I do not pray for Jesus to come as a baby. We do not wait for that first Christmas, for the baby was born two thousand years ago. But we do wait. We wait, we long, we pray for his return. Precisely because Jesus has promised, "Yes, I am coming soon", we pray "Amen. Come, Lord Jesus" (Revelation 22 v 20). Every time we pray, "Your kingdom come" in the Lord's prayer, we are yearning for Jesus to return. We pray for many things; we hope for all manner of blessings; we yearn for answers to many petitions. But above and beyond them all we must give ourselves to urgent prayer, day and night, that Jesus will return soon.

SING

The King shall come, when morning dawns
And light triumphant breaks,
When beauty gilds the eastern hills
And life to joy awakes.

He who was born a little child
To suffer and to die
Shall come with glory, like the sun
That lights the morning sky.

Far brighter than that glorious morn
Shall this fair morning be,
When Christ our King in beauty comes,
And we his face shall see!

The King shall come, when morning dawns
And light and beauty brings.
Hail, Christ the Lord! Your people pray,
"Come quickly, King of kings."
                    (John Brownlie, 1857-1925)

PRAY

O God, who sent your blessed Son into the world to be the Saviour of sinners, and have promised that he will come again to be our Judge: we ask you to increase in us the spirit of watchfulness and prayer, that in the day of his appearing the lamps of our spirit may be trimmed and burning, and we may enter with joy into the marriage supper of the Lamb. We ask it for Jesus' sake, Amen.

JOURNAL

_____

_____

_____

_____

_____

_____

_____

_____

_____

_____

_____

_____

_____

_____

LUKE 2 v 38

38 Coming up to them at that very moment, [Anna] gave thanks to God and spoke about the child to all who were looking forward to the redemption of Jerusalem.

23

WAITING TOGETHER

Waiting can be lonely. It can feel as if everyone around us is moving forward, while we're left behind with an invisible ache: stuck, powerless, waiting. It is such a help to wait with others. That is true of waiting in this life, for the little rescues—jobs, healing, restored relationships, and so on. How much more true is it of waiting for Jesus to return: the big rescue.

We discover today something we might never have guessed: there's a little community of believers in Jerusalem, all waiting for the Messiah. Along with the Best Supporting Actor (Simeon) and the Best Supporting Actress (Anna), there's a group of Best Supporting Extras. Simeon stands with Mary and Joseph; he holds the baby in his arms; and "at that very moment" Anna, this lovely elderly widow, comes up to them. Picture the scene: an older man, a very old woman, the young couple, the baby—a poignant and moving scene in the middle of the busy temple courts. Simeon has spoken, in praise of God and then very personally to Mary. Now Anna gives thanks to God for this child.

And then we discover that there are others there listening: "all who were looking forward to the redemption of Jerusalem". The redemption of Jerusalem means much the same as "the consolation of Israel" in verse 25. It's shorthand for when God fulfils all his old-covenant promises: when he sends the Messiah, his King in David's line, to rescue his people and rule the world.

Who were all these people, gathered there to listen to Anna? We don't know. But they seem to have gathered around Mary and Joseph, Simeon, Anna and the baby as though it was a natural thing. I wonder if they met regularly to pray. Perhaps they booked a room in the temple courts. I expect they were regarded as eccentric by the rich Sadducees, the privileged priests and others, as they insisted on praying and waiting and waiting and hoping that God would send his Messiah. And yet here they are at this wonderful moment, gathered around as this aged widow speaks to them about this child.

Waiting is hard. But these men and women strengthened one another's resolve. When one wavered, another would encourage and cheer them to keep praying. And then, when another's faith faltered, others would remind them of the promises of God. And so, through all the ups and downs of the years, they waited together.

We too are a waiting people; we are not just a collection of expectant individuals. Paul writes to the church in Thessalonica that they "turned to God from idols to serve the living and true God, and to wait for his Son from heaven, whom he raised from the dead—Jesus, who rescues us from the coming wrath" (1 Thessalonians 1 v 9-10).

One good answer to the question "What sort of a church are you? Who are you?" is to say, "We are a community of men and women who are waiting for Jesus to return". Not waiting passively, as if we just wait and never do anything; no, that would be nonsense! But waiting actively—working at our daily work, loving God, loving people, giving our lives for Jesus and his gospel, and all the time praying, "Your kingdom come; come, Lord Jesus!" As we do so, we will never be satisfied by what this world offers, never too disappointed when we do not experience healing or reconciliation or happiness in this life, always keeping our hopes set on that great future day.

So today, remember that gathering around Anna, Simeon, Mary, Joseph and, above all, Jesus—those nameless men and women looking forward to the day when God would fulfil his promises. As Anna speaks to them about this child, they too know that their waiting is not in vain. Let their fulfilled waiting encourage you in your yet-to-be-fulfilled longing for Jesus to return. Keep waiting. Keep strengthening one another's hands in God as you wait together. Look out for the brother or sister whose faith is struggling, who wonders if they can go on waiting. Tell them they can. Pray for them, as they pray for you.

ᶜSING

Yet with the woes of sin and strife
The world has suffered long;
Beneath the angel-strain have rolled
Two thousand years of wrong;
And man, at war with man, hears not
The love-song which they bring;
O hush the noise, ye men of strife,
And hear the angels sing.

And ye, beneath life's crushing load,
Whose forms are bending low,
Who toil along the climbing way
With painful steps and slow,
Look now! for glad and golden hours
Come swiftly on the wing.
O rest beside the weary road,
And hear the angels sing!

For lo! the days are hastening on,
By prophet bards foretold,
When with the ever-circling years
Comes round the age of gold,
When peace shall over all the earth
Its ancient splendours fling,
And the whole world give back the song
Which now the angels sing.
                    (Edmund Hamilton Sears, 1810-1876)

PRAY

Gracious God, who put it into the heart of those men and women two thousand years ago to encourage one another to wait in believing hope, grant us, we pray, to belong to a fellowship of believers who will stir up one another to keep waiting, keep believing, keep hoping and keep praying for Jesus to return, as he surely will. We ask it for Jesus' sake, Amen.

JOURNAL

_____

_____

_____

_____

_____

_____

_____

_____

_____

_____

_____

_____

_____

LUKE 2 v 39-40, 51-52

39 When Joseph and Mary had done everything required by the Law of the Lord, they returned to Galilee to their own town of Nazareth.
40 And the child grew and became strong; he was filled with wisdom, and the grace of God was on him.

[And then, after the story of the twelve-year-old Jesus in the temple]

51 Then [Jesus] went down to Nazareth with [his parents] and was obedient to them. But his mother treasured all these things in her heart. 52 And Jesus grew in wisdom and stature, and in favour with God and man.

24
THE SILENT YEARS

What would it have been like to watch Jesus of Nazareth grow up? I guess we have all watched children grow up. They may be children of friends, or nephews and nieces, or maybe our own sons and daughters. Perhaps at Christmas we tell stories: "I remember when so-and-so was two. Do you remember what she said?" "You know that time when you were seven and you..." And we smile or we laugh, or sometimes we cry. We know what it is to see a boy or girl grow from a newborn baby sleeping to beginning to look around with wide eyes, to beginning to crawl; first steps, first words, toilet-training, tantrums; learning to read, to run, to quarrel, to smile, to grumble, to become good at this, not so good at that, all the way to adulthood.

But what about Jesus? For our final meditation I want us to think—paradoxically—about the thirty years of Jesus' life about which we know next to nothing. All we have are these three verses and the short account in between from when Jesus was twelve. Those thirty years between Jesus' birth and the start of his public ministry account for ninety percent of his life on earth, yet only about one per cent of Luke's Gospel (and less than a half of one per cent of all the Gospels). Compared to the overwhelming detail about the final week of Jesus' life, this is quite a contrast.

The first thing we notice from these verses is that Jesus "grew and became strong"; he "grew in ... stature" (v 40, 52). He developed as children do. He grew up physically. He learned to crawl and walk, he was toilet-trained, he grew taller and stronger. He grew up mentally. He learned to speak and read and reason. He learned the skills of a carpenter. He grew emotionally; he learned to feel and express his feelings. There was nothing non-human about him, for he was and is fully human. No one looked at him and thought they were watching an alien.

Then we notice that he was obedient to Mary and Joseph, as the fifth commandment told him to be. This tiny insight into his godliness as a boy is but the tip of a great iceberg of obedience to all the commandments. And he grew in wisdom; twice Luke tells us this. He learned to behave as the wise person in the book of Proverbs. Try reading through Proverbs, perhaps in January, and see how the wise man there is a portrait of Jesus as he grew. "The fear of the LORD is the beginning of wisdom" (Proverbs 9 v 10); at the root of Jesus' childhood was a deep and loving reverence for God his

Father. That reverence issued in a life of wise words, wise hopes, wise desires, wise deeds. He learned to work hard, to speak kindly and truthfully, to be trustworthy, to be pure sexually, to trust God for everything.

And he grew in grace, or "favour", with God and people. God the Father smiled on this boy as he grew. And—for the moment at least—many people smiled on him too. There was something deeply and humanly attractive about him. He was strong without thoughtlessness. Sensitive without weakness. Angry at injustice but devoid of selfish rage. Active but not self-reliant. Prayerful but not passive. In every respect the boy Jesus demonstrated a perfect and balanced human life. Here is humanity as we were meant to be: the perfect image and likeness of God.

It was very wonderful and deeply attractive. But here is the thought I want to leave with you: consider how much it mattered that Jesus grew like this. The words "I desire to do your will, my God" (Psalm 40 v 8) are a perfect expression of every day, every night, every hour, every year of Jesus' life (Hebrews 10 v 7). At no point—in no nanosecond of Jesus' infancy, boyhood or adult life—did he even so much as desire to do anything other than the perfect will of his Father God. His fully human will was aligned by his own free choice with the will of God his Father, the will of his own divine nature, the will of the Holy Spirit. To us it is almost unimaginable that a full human being could live such a life. And yet he did.

And it mattered. For had he, even for one instant, turned away in rebellion, yearned for some ungodly thing, cherished some impure thought, coveted something that was not his—even just for one moment—then he could not have been our Saviour. To be the sacrifice that paid the penalty for sinners, he had to be flawless. And he was. So, as we leave these Advent meditations, let us take with us a deep sense of wonder at the beautiful and matchless life that Jesus lived for us.

SING

> *He came down to earth from heaven,*
> *Who is God and Lord of all;*
> *And his shelter was a stable*
> *And his cradle was a stall:*
> *With the poor and meek and lowly*
> *Lived on earth our Saviour holy.*
>
> *And through all his perfect childhood,*
> *Day by day like us he grew;*
> *He was little, weak and helpless;*
> *Tears and smiles like us he knew;*
> *And he feels for all our sadness,*
> *And he shares in all our gladness.*
>   (Cecil Frances Alexander, 1818-1895)

PRAY

God our Father, who made humankind to be your likeness upon earth, we praise you that in your Son, the Lord Jesus Christ, we gaze upon that likeness in shining perfection. We adore this flawless Jesus, who lived such a life of unbending devotion to you, so that he might give his life as our perfect sacrifice and Saviour. We thank you that his was indeed a perfect childhood and a sinless life, and all for us. And we thank you in Jesus' name, Amen.

JOURNAL

_____

_____

_____

_____

_____

_____

_____

_____

_____

_____

_____

_____

_____

_____

_____

_____

_____

COMPANY

BIBLICAL | RELEVANT | ACCESSIBLE

At The Good Book Company, we are dedicated to helping Christians and local churches grow. We believe that God's growth process always starts with hearing clearly what he has said to us through his timeless word—the Bible.

Ever since we opened our doors in 1991, we have been striving to produce Bible-based resources that bring glory to God. We have grown to become an international provider of user-friendly resources to the Christian community, with believers of all backgrounds and denominations using our books, Bible studies, devotionals, evangelistic resources, and DVD-based courses.

We want to equip ordinary Christians to live for Christ day by day, and churches to grow in their knowledge of God, their love for one another, and the effectiveness of their outreach.

Call us for a discussion of your needs or visit one of our local websites for more information on the resources and services we provide.

Your friends at The Good Book Company

thegoodbook.com | thegoodbook.co.uk
thegoodbook.com.au | thegoodbook.co.nz
thegoodbook.co.in